CREATIVE
HOMEOWNER®

Best *Signature* Kitchens

CREATIVE HOMEOWNER®, Upper Saddle River, New Jersey

First published in book form in 2009 by

CRE⌂TIVE
HOMEOWNER®

A Division of Federal Marketing Corp.
Upper Saddle River, NJ

Text and photos © 2008 Magnolia Media Group

Signature Kitchens & Baths Magazine is published by Magnolia Media Group

VICE PRESIDENT & PUBLISHER: Timothy O. Bakke
MANAGING EDITOR: Fran J. Donegan
ART DIRECTOR: David Geer
PRODUCTION COORDINATOR: Sara M. Markowitz
DIGITAL IMAGING SPECIALIST: Frank Dyer

Current Printing (last digit)
10 9 8 7 6 5 4 3 2

Manufactured in the United States of America

Best Signature Kitchens
Library of Congress Control Number: 2008941322
ISBN-10: 1-58011-455-5
ISBN-13: 978-1-58011-455-4

CREATIVE HOMEOWNER®
A Division of Federal Marketing Corp.
24 Park Way
Upper Saddle River, NJ 07458
www.creativehomeowner.com

CONTENTS

SOME BASICS

open house   **6**
Why a kitchen-great room combination makes sense.

sustaining growth   **10**
It's easy being green in the kitchen.

in good company   **14**
Welcome your guests into the kitchen.

it's a classic   **18**
Use these tips to create a timeless look.

THE KITCHENS

cook's delight   **22**
An expanded kitchen pleases a cooking couple.

room to breathe   **24**
A front-of-home kitchen makes a great first impression.

room for family   **26**
Three small rooms become one spacious kitchen.

a refreshing palette   **28**
A homeowner's pool inspires a soothing color scheme.

an eye on design   **30**
This plan overlooks the family room—and the kids.

grand openings   **32**
Bigger is better for these homeowners.

space for all   **34**
A 40-year-old kitchen gets a much-needed remodel.

functional elegance   **36**
Special meals for family and friends inspired this plan.

at home in nyc   **38**
A city kitchen gets an elegant makeover.

bungalow style   **40**
This new kitchen has vintage character.

one of a kind   **42**
Exotic veneered cabinets add wow to a design.

old is new again   **44**
A new kitchen dramatically transforms an older home.

pinnacle of design   **46**
A great design takes advantage of a cathedral ceiling.

maximizing marvel   48
A custom kitchen suits the needs and desires of its owners.

clad in class   50
Good-looking furniture-style cabinets conceal appliances.

fit for a family   52
Multiple work zones accommodate a large family.

asian aesthetic   54
East meets West in this inspired design.

historically home   56
A new kitchen retains Victorian references.

deliciously detailed   58
Luscious colors and inviting curves make this room cozy.

the right angles   60
This timber-frame home's kitchen has personality plus.

sleek stylings   62
Outstanding materials add flair to a compact design.

room with a view   64
An uptown look restores a kitchen with downtown views.

seaside serenity   66
A crisp white cottage kitchen suits its beach house.

artistic flair   68
This kitchen stimulates the eye and the appetite.

modern cucina   70
Borrow adjacent space to enlarge a small kitchen.

mountain getaway   72
Color and handsome cabinets add visual impact.

simple comfort   74
Upgrading an old kitchen boosts function and looks.

california cucina   76
Removing a wall brightens a townhouse kitchen.

perfect triangle   78
Proper scale and proportion improves a large layout.

triumphal arches   80
Beautiful details accent an Old World-inspired look.

culinary sophisticate   82
A crowded galley kitchen becomes an open, airy space.

bright ideas   84
Reconfiguring walls and cabinets lets in the sun.

functional elegance   86
Sleek ideas cater to an entertaining family of four.

soothing style   88
Simplicity defines this pleasingly functional design.

bella cucina   90
Fantastic Tuscan styling fulfills a homeowner's dream.

cozy condo   92
A walk-in closet becomes an exceptional kitchen.

modern motives   94
Traditional and modern elements mix with panache.

big apple cookery   96
User-friendly features make a city kitchen enjoyable.

ample antiquity   98
An Old World design meets modern needs.

artistic in asheville   100
A designer mixes art and architecture for pizzazz.

heart of the home   102
A handsome island serves as a stunning focal point.

beaming with beauty   104
Post-and-beam construction uplifts a kitchen.

at its best   106
A designer reorganizes a kitchen for improved function.

stylish solutions   108
A small den and kitchen become a culinary treat.

tidy in tennessee   110
This functional design doesn't look like a work space.

open and functional   112
A family kitchen gets a makeover.

island paradise   114
The benefits of removing walls and raising the ceiling.

dazzling design   116
Two cooks get the space they need and a look they love.

high stylings   118
Uncompromising homeowners have it their way.

slim to stunning   120
Smart organization makes the most of a floor plan.

spaciously updated   122
A redesign preserves the essence of a Modern classic.

flattering imitation   124
A mother-in-law's kitchen inspired this grand creation.

storage galore   126
Great cabinetry is key to this kitchen's success.

expanded elegance   128
The whole family gets into the act in this enlarged space.

space with grace   130
A redesigned layout produces a family's dream kitchen.

strong storage   132
Load-bearing solutions support this remodeled room.

a catered affair   134
This kitchen caters to a social couple's lifestyle.

tuscany at topsail   136
Northern-Italian influences spice up this design.

views of villagio   138
Old and new mix to create a very personal space.

open and bright   140
New cream-color cabinets brighten a dark, dated kitchen.

white at home   142
A neutral scheme and lots of glass open up this design.

set in stone   144
A handsome stone wall adds a strong textural quality.

designer's dream   146
Tasteful details flavor this designer's kitchen.

chef's convenience   148
This kitchen caters to the person who does the cooking.

timeless design   150
An open configuration has appealing views.

entertaining with ease   152
This remodeled kitchen is fit for a gourmand.

function and flair   154
Victorian-style cabinets blend with antique furnishings.

pretty in pembroke   156
Better-organized work space suits a family's lifestyle.

passing through   158
A pass-through opens a kitchen to the dining room.

wine and dine   160
How to outfit a kitchen, Napa Valley style.

elegant simplicity   162
Rich hues embue a dream kitchen with warmth.

fantasy island   164
A spacious island anchors this enlarged kitchen.

sparing no expense   166
Only the best was good enough for these homeowners.

spanish hacienda   168
This renovated kitchen has a rustic, Old World flavor.

contempo cucina   170
A Colonial-style home gets a modern kitchen.

kosher style   172
A designer responds to an observant family's request.

grand comfort   174
Elaborate elements elevate a culinary space.

a family affair   176
This kitchen pleases a multigenerational household.

winning recipe   178
A knockout design adds square feet and extra storage.

creative corbels   180
Decorative architectural trimwork refines a new kitchen.

old world design   182
Opulent styling lavishes a kitchen with European charm.

entertaining oasis   184
An open floor plan welcomes weekend guests.

twice as nice   186
How to add extra warmth to a contemporary kitchen.

flying high   188
A designer interprets a homeowner's request.

lake activity   190
A remodeling opens a kitchen to a lake view.

open invitation   192
This transformed space is ready for entertaining.

a new era   194
A working couple updates a 1918 kitchen.

double the assets   196
A paneled barrel ceiling gives this kitchen a unique look.

savvy storage   198
Simple cabinets respect a kitchen's uncomplicated lines.

modern luxury   200
Contemporary Italian cabinets inspire a kitchen design.

old world elegance   202
European styling coordinates with a home's features.

tuscan triumph   204
New owners reinvent the kitchen in a grand home.

complete treatment   206
Lifting the ceiling takes a kitchen to new heights.

dimensions of design   208
This new kitchen balances style and function.

warm and bright   210
Expanding into the dining room changes everything.

natural wonder   212
A 1970s kitchen gets a new look.

cozy and bright   214
A redesigned kitchen has cozy, contemporary flair.

radical transformation   216
A better plan serves a young family's needs.

sleek and chic   218
Distinct zones reflect a modern couple's lifestyle.

modern hospitality   220
A new floor plan suits an entertaining family's lifestyle.

points of view   222
Open, interconnected spaces capture exterior views.

designer's challenge   224
Ingenious planning puts storage where it's needed.

grand openings   226
Removing walls creates a contemporary environment.

penthouse view   228
Period details meld with state-of-the-art functionality.

fit for a chef   230
A designer creates a personal kitchen for a pro.

minimalist maven   232
This modern look has lofty ambitions.

wine in the design   234
It's a one-of-a-kind kitchen for two cooks.

fabulous fusion   236
A traditional home gets an efficient modern kitchen.

perfectly positioned   238
Two islands improve cooking and entertaining areas.

OPEN HOUSE

Kitchen–great room combos provide ample area for entertaining and keep the cook connected to the family.

STORY BY **CAMILLE TORRES** // PHOTOS COURTESY OF **JAUREGUI ARCHITECTURE, CONSTRUCTION, INTERIORS**

GONE ARE THE DAYS when a kitchen was relegated to its own end of the house, with only a doorway linking it to other living areas. Instead, open floor plans with a connected kitchen, breakfast nook, and living area are becoming increasingly popular. Homeowners with families or those who like to entertain are turning toward a more fluid arrangement. Creating a gathering space for before, during, and after meals, an open kitchen maintains a sense of togetherness (sans crowding) during day-to-day activities.

"It's very popular to have a triangle of the kitchen, breakfast nook, and family room as almost one space. The majority of our homes are planned that way," says Luis Jauregui, AIA, president of Austin-based Jauregui Architecture, Construction, Interiors. And while it's typical to do a separate dining room and occasionally an additional living room, some homeowners are including even the formal areas in the single area. "We've been doing a lot of homes where the kitchen, two different living areas, and two different eating areas are one large open space," he says. In these plans, the kitchen is open to the entire home, with the exception of the bedrooms and office. "People are beginning to see that when the formal living and dining rooms are segregated, they can't be enjoyed as much," Jauregui adds.

Bringing the formal spaces under the umbrella of the informal allows more flexibility and maximizes the use of space. In smaller homes, these areas can be incorporated, rather than eliminated, allowing family and friends to gather in a large room. "It's great for saving space and trying to economize, but on the homes we're doing it has nothing to do with economy. It's just the way people like to live," Jauregui says. And the requests are increasing for such homes, especially for empty nesters who appreciate the openness during holidays and family gatherings. It's also ideal for those who enjoy entertaining informally for large groups. Clusters of guests can mingle in different areas without feeling disconnected from the party, and the kitchen can be the hub of activity without being overcrowded.

But creating an open kitchen-living

Left: Eye-pleasing columns and a lower ceiling height set apart the kitchen without dividing it from the living area. Right: A chandelier provides identity for an otherwise undefined open eating area.

area isn't without its challenges. Because a kitchen is such a highly functional space, all its exposed elements can be less than aesthetically pleasing. To help it blend with the other areas, utilize architectural and interior treatments—like panels that camouflage appliances or cabinetry that blends with living room built-ins—that can be appreciated one or two rooms over. "Marry form and function," Jauregui advises, "not allowing function to outweigh aesthetics and vice versa."

Also keep in mind window locations and doors that open to outdoor spaces. Make sure that traffic can flow smoothly outside for combination indoor-outdoor entertaining. With proper design, a patio can become part of the great room. Strategic window placement also ensures that natural light illuminates most of the kitchen-living-area spaces.

An additional challenge to great room design is acoustics. If the ceiling treatment is too large and flat, every sound amplifies.

Break the ceilings with architectural elements such as beams. This will also improve the overall appearance. Make sure that you have ample furniture placed throughout the connecting rooms to help absorb sound. If there are hardwood or tile floors throughout, incorporate rugs and softer materials.

To keep the great room from looking like one vast expanse, create niches and carve out smaller task-based spaces within the overall area. This can be done in part through ceiling variants. One large space, like the family room, can have a higher ceiling height, with lower ceilings in the other areas. Dually accomplishing separation and connection, homeowners can have a large living area that is open to food-oriented appendices. The result is spaces that feel more intimate but are still a part of the overall area.

Groupings of furniture around a fireplace and/or television give owners and guests different seating options. In the kitchen, a center food-prep island improves functionality, while a small area for a built-in desk provides organization for recipes and bills. In the dining area, some homeowners are opting for a wine room or wet bar. According to Jauregui, "This creates a more challenging equation for the architect and interior designer in combining the multiplicity of the spaces, but a good architect can do it."

To keep the different areas from looking too disjointed, unify the aesthetics with such elements as matching texture, color, flooring, and/or trim work. Jauregui suggests using wood in the different spaces. Areas can be tied together or differentiated with variations in the stains or colors of the wood. Similarities in windows and window treatments can also draw the areas together.

Although the different settings should flow together visually, there needs to be good zoning of the spaces. Furniture is a great tool to use to create delineation without separation. Keep the color scheme similar in all the niches but utilize different sizes and styles of pieces. More formal furnishings can decorate one area, whereas casual elements fill another. A long sofa or a chair/side-table combo can also be used to semi-divide rooms. A counter with bar stools where the kitchen and living room meet is a popular option. Near a window, a small table with a casual chandelier above it identifies the breakfast nook, whereas across the room a larger table, area rug, and elaborate chandelier indicate formal dining.

Large case openings, archways, and columns also are great tools to define spaces without cutting them from the overall area. Lighting fixtures like pendants, chandeliers, and sconces can help differentiate spaces as well.

Be sure that each of the areas within the overall space has an identity. For example, make a statement with the dining table but choose chairs that follow the overall color palette. Television and media are typically a large component in the family room, so allow them to be a part of the architectural statement. "With open spaces, you can use a larger media center that you can enjoy from multiple space, and you can also create spaces where you don't want to look at the TV," Jauregui says.

Hearths are similarly helpful in defining an area. "Fireplaces are one thing I love about an open plan. You get the enjoyment of being in one space and having so much available to

your eyes," Jauregui says. "Fireplaces can be a beautiful area as an accent point or terminus visually. They can be a very large, dominant statement or small and quaint as part of a breakfast or dining area."

Nearby, a vertical vent hood architecturally mirrors a fireplace while serving as a focal point for the kitchen. Conversely, homeowners can minimize or de-emphasize the hood if they want the room to blend more with the other areas. "There are no hard rules but a lot of opportunities," Jauregui notes.

But no matter what opportunity you opt for, make sure that you have a good relationship with your architect and interior designer to ensure they incorporate your likes and avoid your dislikes. According to Jauregui, "The input of the architect and how he/she translates the client's persona is an important element to draw the spaces together." Since the combined kitchen and great room is where you and your family will spend the majority of your time, above all, it should express your personality and make you and your guests feel comfortable.

Furniture, such as this sofa and bar seating, subtly separates the spaces for various functions, while a neutral color scheme unifies the area.

SUSTAINING GROWTH

With the medley of choices to green your home environment, creating a healthy, earth–conscious design in the kitchen or bath is easier than ever before.

:: STORY BY SILVER HOGUE

As environmentally friendly lifestyles become more popular, eco-savvy designers and manufacturers are striving to create sustainable products that bring out the greener side of every room in the home. And in the kitchen and bath, the sustainable selection is growing faster than ever.

THAT'S A BRIGHT IDEA An ecologically conscious quick-change artist, energy-efficient lighting in the kitchen and bath takes on many forms. Tom Hatch, lead architect at Hatch Partnership in Austin, Texas, suggests installing dimmer switches, which allow for lower lighting levels and save about 40 percent on normal lighting costs. Dimmer switches also extend the life of bulbs. According to Hatch, when dimming the lights by half, bulbs last about 20 times longer and need to be changed less frequently. Hatch says installing occupancy sensor switches is another efficient way to save energy. Used most frequently in bathrooms, closets and garages, the hands-free technology automatically turns lights on and off when one enters or exits a room.

Of course, just switching to a non-incandescent bulb can also work wonders, reducing the energy output in mass quantities. According to Energy Star, Americans would save about $8 billion each year in energy costs if they replaced their five most frequently used light fixtures or bulbs with environmentally sound models. Lighting can make up 25 percent of one's electric bill and lighting control systems are a luminous way to reap significant savings.

ATTAINABLE SUSTAINABLE While lighting is an important element, it's only one of several ways to environmentally outfit the kitchen and bath areas of the home. Many homeowners are finding new ways to use recycled products in both spaces. The growing inventory includes such elements as glass tiles made from recycled bottles, countertops made from waste paper, cloth fibers, glass, cement, aluminum, and reused glass, fiberboard panels made from recycled paper and flooring made from a quickly renewing resource like bamboo.

According to Lisa DiMartino, vice president of marketing for Seattle-based Environmental Home Center, preliminary versions of these products were not well received because they were plagued by performance problems and looked too "earthy." She says if products such as these are going to enjoy mass appeal, they have to look good. Fortunately, recycled products have improved in performance and appearance and have taken on a certain cachet with the environmentally aware.

An example of this more natural approach is the incorporation of unusual paper materials

MORE THAN MEETS THE EYE

This kitchen may appear to be just another pretty face, but hidden in it are plenty of eco-friendly additions.

» Each of the cabinets are re-faced with salvaged—rather than newly harvested—maple

» All appliances are energy efficient

» The flooring is sustainably harvested maple flooring

» Venetian Plaster backsplash, made of durable, natural lime plaster

such as ShetkaStone for cabinet doors and moldings. The solid-surface material is fabricated from wastepaper, plant and cloth fibers. Manufactured by New Prague, Minnesota-based All Paper Recycling, ShetkaStone comes in any color and can be sawed, sanded, glued, nailed, or screwed and finished with any wood or stone sealant. The company also manufactures ShetkaStone countertops that are waterproof and can accept an undermount sink. Other paper-based counters include PaperStone and Richlite, both of which accept undermount sinks as well.

Other natural products include Brooklyn-based IceStone's recycled-glass countertop surfacing product, which is made of 75 percent recycled glass and cement and is suitable for floors, walls and counters. Other companies such as American Terrazzo of Garland, Texas, sell an epoxy resin product called EnviroGlas Terrazzo that contains recycled glass. According to company president Tim Whaley, the material is designed for floors and countertops and resists

chemicals and bacterial growth.

Energy-efficient appliances also make a great alternative to traditional choices, without giving up on power and cleaning capability. Fagor dishwashers allow you to conserve energy with an option to regulate load size, while sensors determine the exact amount of water needed per load, so neither water nor energy is wasted. Bosch offers the EnergyStar qualified Evolution 800, which features external controls, reducing the need to open the door to maintain a constant temperature inside the fridge. A gentle door alarm also prevents energy waste and keeps foods from spoiling.

EVERY DROP COUNTS Green manufacturers now offer products such as water-saving faucets, organic towels and shower curtains, all-green cleaning products and a smorgasbord of organic toiletries. But the shower and toilet are two of the easiest and most cost-effective places to decrease your environmental

footprint. An inefficient showerhead can use 20 to 30 liters of water each minute, while an efficient one will give high-quality showers using only nine liters, according to the Ecological Homes Web site, an Australian-based company that provides information to individuals wanting to make their homes more sustainable. Many environmentally sound showerheads come with additional features including massage, self-cleaning and flow cut-off control.

According to Lloyd Hathcock, chairman of the Water Conservation Division of the American Water Works Association, old, inefficient toilets are responsible for most of the water wasted in American homes. Hathcock says replacing these toilets with EPA WaterSense-labeled toilets could save approximately two billion gallons of water per day across the country. If a family of four replaced a 3.5-gallon-per-flush toilet, made between 1980 and 1994, with a WaterSense-labeled toilet, it could save more than $90 annually on its water bill and $2,000 over the lifetime of the toilet, according to William Cutler, president of Niagara Conservation. Cutler says with these savings, a new WaterSense-labeled toilet can pay for itself in just a few years.

IT'S A MATERIAL WORLD Choosing organic and/or earth-friendly alternatives to such items as shower curtains and bath towels is another healthy option. Organic materials such as hemp, natural cotton and wool are chemical-free and less abrasive to the skin. According to some manufacturers, it's also a healthier option for people with allergies, multiple chemical sensitivities and skin problems.

Organic products are also void of harmful polluting chemicals, which makes them more sustainable.

According to a report by the California Sustainable Cotton Project, chemical-free, organic cotton, wool and hemp offer safe, sensible home furnishing alternatives. Wool is naturally resistant to odors, mildew and dust mites, which can be another source of allergies. Hemp fabric is generally more durable and less environmentally taxing than conventional cotton or synthetics.

Los Angeles eco-designer Kelly LaPlante, owner of Organic Interior Design, says whether it's organic materials and soy candles, or paints with a low volume of volatile organic compounds, you don't have to sacrifice style when you choose organic and sustainable products for the kitchen and bath. LaPlante says in her extensive search for sustainable, luxurious and exciting products, one thing holds true: Clients don't have to choose between a healthy planet and a beautiful kitchen and bath. Today, they can have the best of both worlds. «

In Good Company

A kitchen should reflect the needs of a host to the very last detail, and creating a culinary space to welcome a crowd is essential for any avid entertainer.   STORY BY **NICOLE HOLLAND**

Once a utilitarian space banished to relatively cramped quarters away from the household hustle and bustle, the kitchen has transformed into a primary point of convergence. In other words, it's not just for cooking anymore. In fact, these busy rooms are party central in many residences, which means they need to be accommodating to their gracious entertainers, as well as to their grateful guests.

Since the layout is one of the most important factors of the new area, "think about the flow of traffic when designing your kitchen for entertaining," said Erinn Valencich of Omniarte Design. Kitchens hosting informal parties are best suited to an open floor plan,

but the more formal festivities may require a separation between the kitchen and the eating area to keep the activities partitioned. "Guests aren't necessarily seeing the preparation of the meal, but they are there to enjoy the results of that preparation," said Al Curran CKD, WRID, senior designer at Bella Domicile in Madison, Wisconsin. To accommodate this separation, it may be necessary to include additional rooms, beyond a formal dining room, in which to retire after the meal is complete.

For these formal layouts, adding a butler's pantry may also come in handy, from preparing the next course to staging desserts. In the event that caterers are present during

a gathering, the butler's pantry also provides room for meal make-ready and cleanup.

INSULAR IDEAS

There is truly no better space to gather than in the kitchen, next to all the action during a dinner party. The island can truly be the hub of activity in the kitchen, so designing it to work for you is ideal. When everyone is gathered around, it is important to keep lines of sight open in the area. For example, including a cooktop in the center island will prevent the cook from turning his or her back to the guests as the meal is prepared. To the same degree, a vegetable prep sink and undercounter refrigerator will keep everything at an arm's reach and reduce the amount of time spent running around the kitchen.

The undercounter refrigerator is also the perfect place to stow appetizers and beverages, so if your guests are arriving one by one, it's easy to pull out a cold drink for them when they arrive. To augment available workspace, add a snack bar to the island to set out drinks, serve a buffet or have guests pull up a chair and enjoy some bar-style snacking. And don't forget to accessorize the space with a splash of color. "Fresh flowers are also a nice touch in the kitchen," said Valencich. "Most people don't think to accessorize their counters the same way they would do a tabletop."

APPLIANCE UTILITY

Make the kitchen work for you when deciding on the appliances. For instance, a second dishwasher is helpful for getting everything clean and out of the way at once. "You can be running one [dishwasher] with pots and pans and be filling the dirty dishes in the second one, so one does not have to be stacking plates and bowls," said Curran. Also

consider a second oven to ensure that dishes can prepared and completed simultaneously, and for keeping servings and breads toasty, a warming drawer is ideal.

Wine refrigerators aren't just for connoisseurs anymore. Store your best vino in a temperature-controlled setting to ensure freshness and the perfect serving temperature each time. From a six-bottle model to a cooler designed to hold more than 20, finding a space for this appliance will be well worth it. And if guests would prefer a little pick-me-up, offer coffee along with the wine. "An espresso machine built into the wall is also a great party pleaser," said Valencich,

Before the guests arrive, transform the sink into fun focal point by adding refreshments. "I love an entertainment sink," said Valencich. "Kohler has some long narrow ones that are great at parties filled with ice and drinks. Or for a kids' party, fill it with Popsicles and frozen treats."

The island can be the center of attention in the kitchen during a festivity. To keep everything within reach, stock it with amenities, such as a wine cooler, mini refrigerator or second dishwasher.

An open floor plan makes a space easy to navigate and a spacious island offers guests room to gather.

ADDED AMBIANCE

Using lighting techniques when hosting a soiree can help guests feel more relaxed and comfortable and can dictate the mood of the gathering. "Lighting makes all the difference and will really make the kitchen sparkle," said Valenich. "When I'm entertaining I put on the undercabinet lighting and the pendants on a low dimmer—it's really elegant."

TAKE IT OUTSIDE

If you live in a climate where weather permits, some kitchen spaces set up for entertaining have an adjoining exterior space for eating and relaxing. The outdoor living area, garden or deck, sometimes infused with the kitchen space, takes entertainment to the next level. To keep things simplified, ensure easy access between the two culinary spaces. "Not all of your refrigeration needs are going to be taking place outdoors, and you will be transferring meats to the grill, and many times it could be beverages back and forth," said Curran. "You don't want uneven floor material on the exterior of the home." And this is another time to consider traffic patterns in the layout, making sure that there isn't a need to walk through a number of rooms to make it to the outdoor kitchen from the interior.

SMALL PRECAUTIONS

Even though they say entertaining is all about the guests, you still need to keep yourself safe and comfortable in your own space. Make sure to install nonslip flooring in the kitchen and in the hallways leading out to the outdoor living area. In addition to a slip-free surface, keep tired toes happy with a gel mat specifically designed for use in the kitchen. Stain-resistant and durable, they are a soothing relief to aching feet.

Also, take a close look at your hardware before making the final decision, as some shapes may catch or rip clothing. "Sometimes hardware may have an exposed end," said Curran, "so be aware of protrusions that might be sticking out of the cabinetry or from appliances."

No matter if the project is an upgrade or a complete remodel, take your kitchen to the next stratum of socials with a space specially designed to make you, and your guests, comfortable. «

A second oven in or near the kitchen means there's no waiting around during the dinner party. Jenn-Air's Convenience oven bakes, broils, toasts and warms in one easy-to-use unit.

It's a Classic

Banish stale styles from your culinary space with these timeless tips.

STORY BY ALISON RICH : PHOTOGRAPHY BY CHRIS COX

Choose clean and classic looks in not-so-easy to replace elements like cabinetry, flooring and countertops to create a lasting design.

Although it may be tempting to outfit your culinary space with the today's too-cool trendsetting accoutrements, doing so may create a dated disaster down the road. If you have any doubts, just picture the avocado-colored kitchens that were de rigueur several decades back. Even white-washed oak cabinets, the oh-so hot design darlings of the 1980s, have seen their red-hot sizzle turn to unfabulous fizzle. The moral of these telling tales? If they rely totally on up-to-the-minute milieus, cook's nooks run the risk of turning stale long before their owners are ready to reinvest in their redesign. To help ensure their staying power, we enlisted the aid of three trés-talented kitchen creators, who've generously supplied their tips to ensure your eating-and-greeting area is an eye-catching classic.

NOT ACTING ITS AGE Cat Wei, co-host and designer on the DIY Network's "Material Girls," says an ageless aesthetic is all about

Simple updates will keep a kitchen looking fresh. A vibrant wall color or a new set of simple hardware is the ideal addition for an out-of-date space.

being clean, smart and workable. "As the most utilized room in a house, it has to perform but needs to be comfortable or even nurturing," she said. "It's a design that doesn't try too hard and lovingly tells the story of its owners—or the future owners if it's a new house." The context of the abode is another aspect that should shape the space, Wei added. "A small apartment in a city could have a streamlined European look with minimal appliances, while the sprawling house in the country can entertain a large country kitchen with a farmhouse sink and breakfast bar."

Cheryl Daugvila of Cheryl D. & Co. in LaGrange, Ill., agrees. "I always try to tie my designs into the architectural integrity of the home," she said. For example, an ornate country French kitchen probably would not be the right match for a bilevel raised ranch. "If it doesn't go with the house, it's going to stand out drastically," she said. "The style of the house should delegate what the interior should look like."

Another prudent consideration for a time-tested layout: functionality, says Terry Scarborough CMKBD, ASID, designer/

showroom manager at Kitchens By Deane in New Canaan, Conn. "Looks aren't everything," she said. "It's really important that the storage works, that the layout works, that it's safe and meets the needs of the people working in it." And a fully functioning floor plan is poised for a long lifespan, she added. "One of the reasons people want to redo their kitchen is because it doesn't function."

A timeless kitchen inherently sports a design that's difficult to date, so making such minor tweaks as changing the cabinet hardware and repainting the cabinets and the walls— neutrals are always the best bet—are instant brighteners that add spice to the space without compromising its classic look, Daugvila said.

The good news, Scarborough says, is that there is no real strong trend right now, which means that a current creation is more likely to stay fresh for years.

MATERIAL WORLD Just like a book is edited to ensure it flows seamlessly, a kitchen needs some occasional revising to ensure it endures with perpetual elegance and to erase any tell-tale signs of aging.

"Choose simple hardware for cabinets," Wei said. "Anything too ornamental may go out of style." Also, use recessed lights and other simple illumination options and then choose one snazzy fixture to add pizzazz. "For an eat-in kitchen, add the drama in a light fixture over the table," she said. "If you have a bar area, pick pendant lights in clear glass. Colored glass pendants may feel like pub or rec room lighting."

Neutral colors and long-lived woods like cherry and maple are smart choices, Scarborough says, as are cleaner, more classic lines in the paneling and moldings. Daugvila echoes that sentiment: "They're classic and can be refinished or changed in color if need be," noting that classic framed flat-panel cabinetry is a win-win for its here-to-stay ways.

But a dateless design doesn't have to be drab, Scarborough says, noting that homeowners can put in some personality with paint and fabrics, hardware and lighting, which all can easily be modified when it's time for an aesthetic adjustment. The main point to ponder: Opt for classic designs in hard-to-replace kitchen elements like cabinets and countertops and add a splash of flash in the more minor items.

ON THE SURFACE The workhorse of the home, a kitchen constantly is at the receiving end of its fair share of rough-and-tumble wear and tear. As such, it practically begs for materials that can stand up to the abuse. Wei recommends slate and terrazzo for floors. Lavastone, Corian, granite and wood butcher block are tops for counters. "Use quality materials that are natural and solid," she said. "Stay away from laminates and linoleum that can peel and age."

Daugvila, too, recommends tile and any type of solid surface for their stalwartness. "You just have to watch the trendiness if you want it to be timeless," she cautioned. "I swear by wood cabinets because you always have the possibility of refinishing them, touching them up or refreshing them with polishes and waxes."

STAYING ALIVE Although they're au courant today, eco-friendly and natural materials will stick around, thus rendering them worthy timeless-tradition additions, Wei says. Other here-to-stay elements include sustainably

SIDEBAR

Heed these spot-on tips to ensure your design isn't short-lived.

1. Don't use exotic woods like zebrawood or santos mahogany. They aren't eco-friendly and are of the moment but not much more. *CW*

2. Bamboo might be eco-friendly but has a very specific look that may not age well. *CW*

3. Keep accents to a minimum. *CW*

4. Moroccan tiles, back-painted glass, ceramic or glass tiles are all great choices but require a commitment so keep colors neutral. *CW*

5. To seal and protect natural stone, use a penetrating silicone-based sealer. For wood, use tung oil for a semi-matte finish. *CW*

6. Take a cue from Mother Nature; her colors don't fade and are never trendy. Avoid the 1970s combo of yellow and brown and opt for more neutral and natural colorations. *CW*

7. Hardware and molding details can date a kitchen. "'Keep it smart and simple' has always been my opinion, and put enough [detail] in to make an impact without overdoing it." *CD*

8. Consider furniture styles that are classics. *CD*

9. Choose your backsplash carefully because it's more difficult to replace. Simpler is better. *TS*

10. Incorporate cabinets with classic detailing. Avoid overly decorative added-on elements like cathedral-arched doors and heavy applied molding details. And steer clear of trendy colors in elements such as counters and cabinets that are tougher—and pricier—to change. *TS*

managed or responsibly harvested woods, recycled glass tiles, lava stone and materials that are natural but not necessarily green. As for appliances, stainless steel is here to stay, especially in professional-grade or industrial-looking styles, Wei says. Scarborough agrees. "It's been here forever," she said. "And I think it's going to be around forever and is certainly a safer bet than colored appliances." Open layouts that overflow into other living spaces—a plan perfect for entertaining—also are everlasting, Wei notes.

Fashioning an undatable design doesn't mean you can't create an out-of-the-ordinary mélange, Daugvila says. "If you want something timeless," she said, "sometimes you have to step outside your comfort zone and look at other styles that are going to be the classics." «

Cook's Delight

THIS PROJECT IN SEDALIA, COLORADO, was a major renovation, which included an addition to expand the kitchen. The biggest challenge was the need to create practical work zones within the grand space. Also, the layout had to accommodate both husband and wife, as both are cooks and wanted separate cooking areas.

To meet the desires of the client, Jill Ellis of Colorado Kitchen Designs, working with Tom Owens of Creative Remodeling, provided dual dishwashers, sinks, cooktop and ovens for each area, making it possible for both cooks to be at work at the same time. And since the couple's large extended family visits the country home regularly, there needed to be plenty of room to enjoy the meals they prepared. A large, free form raised wood bar top on the island provides enough seating for several people. In addition, multiple levels on the island make entertaining a breeze.

On these festive occasions separate "buffet" areas provide the perfect location for serving food. The space also features a warming drawer, steam oven and convection oven to ensure any dish is prepared to perfection. A stainless steel island sink and stainless refrigerator provide eye-catching additions to the space, tying together all the room's elements into one satisfying design. «

DESIGNER
Jill Ellis
Colorado Kitchen
Designs, LLC
5475 Leetsdale Drive,
Ste. 200
Denver, CO 80246
303.321.4410

SPECIAL FEATURES
Multiple levels on island; hand-made custom copper hood and sink in his-and-her kitchen zones; leathered granite; two different finishes on cabinetry; raised bar made from Reclaimed Elm

DIMENSIONS
29' x 19'

PRODUCTS USED
Cabinetry: Wood Harbor
Flooring: Reclaimed oak
Countertops: Leathered Juperana Antico Granite
Sink(s): Custom copper, primary; stainless steel, island
Faucets: Hans Grohe
Dishwasher: Bosch
Cooktop: Wolf
Rangetop: Viking
Refrigerator: Maytag
Wallcovering: Paint
Oven: Miele
Warming drawer: Miele
Microwave: Miele
Steam oven/convection oven: Miele

PHOTOGRAPHER: TIM MURPHY

Room to Breathe

THE KITCHEN OF THIS LOVELY COLORADO TOWNHOME is situated immediately in front of the home's entrance, which means it plays an important role in the look and feel of the dwelling. The homeowners felt the kitchen's layout was creating some serious problems, so they called upon Jill B. Ellis of Colorado Kitchen Designs LLC to remedy the situation.

The homeowners' main goal was to open their kitchen to the rest of their living space, while still maintaining some separation from the front door. The problem with this was a solid wall between the front entrance and the kitchen, which created a closed-in feeling. To combat the problem, Ellis reduced the length of the wall by half and created a furniture hutch piece to take its place. The hutch has glass doors on both sides, as well as interior lighting that shines though the cabinets and creates a brilliant effect that can be seen from the front entrance.

To incorporate the kitchen into the rest of the home, Ellis placed an additional glass-fronted display unit beneath a structural beam. An eating bar also lengthens the kitchen space, while providing a place to dine and view the flat-screen television. A tumbled marble backsplash and golden granite countertops tie the kitchen in with the rest of the home, without the room being the first thing visitors notice when they walk through the front door. «

DESIGNER
Jill B. Ellis
Colorado Kitchen
Designs LLC
5475 Leetsdale Drive
Suite 200
Denver, CO 80246
303.321.4410

SPECIAL FEATURES
Multilevel peninsula;
pillow stone tile
backsplash; leaded glass;
glass hutch

DIMENSIONS
15 x 9

PRODUCTS USED
Cabinetry: Holiday
Kitchens
Flooring: Wood
Countertops: Granite
Dishwasher: KitchenAid
Range: GE Profile
Refrigerator: GE Profile
Microwave: GE
Advantium
Ventilation: Vent-A-Hood

MEMBER OF
SEN DESIGN GROUP

PHOTOGRAPHER: PHILLIP NILSSON

Room for Family

THIS HOMEOWNER IN Pittsburgh, Pennsylvania, had three small, disjointed rooms, so the challenge in this space was opening up these nooks so that family could cook and commune with each other.

Construction preparation was extensive. Mary Jane Iksic of Creative Kitchens and More Inc. removed two walls to open up the space and allow the expanded room to come alive. The walls that were removed were bearing walls, and the designer had to do extensive—and creative!—work to ensure the home was sufficiently supported post-removal. For example, one of the ornate pillars in the center island hides a support for the bearing wall.

Mary Jane and the construction supervisor, George Iksic, combined talents to design an island that worked to hide a main support column effectively and discreetly. The main angled island with a sink and raised eating space was to be the centerpiece of the design, and George incorporated structural elements that made it both feasible and fashionable.

Now, multiple cooks can use the kitchen, and there is plenty of space for separate prep and use areas. The flow from other areas of the house also is vastly improved. In the end, the designer incorporated every element on the client's wish list and the homeowners were overjoyed. «

DESIGNER
Mary Jane Iksic
Creative Kitchens and
More Inc.
668 Pittsburgh Road
Butler, PA 16002
724.586.2148

SPECIAL FEATURES
Two islands; wood-
paneled refrigerator;
prep areas for multiple
cooks

DIMENSIONS
27 x 23

PRODUCTS USED
Cabinetry: Kabinart,
maple paint with glaze
and cherry island
Flooring: Porcelain tile,
Chateau Lyon
Countertops: Hanstone
by Blume's
Sink(s): Blanco
Faucets: Danze
Refrigerator: Jenn-Air
Microwave drawer: Sharp

A Refreshing Palette

THIS POOL HOUSE kitchen needed to make a splash, so the Scarborough, Georgia, homeowners called on Mary Ann Cullens Franklin, CKD, of Designs by Five Inc. to create it. The clients requested a very monochromatic color palette that would feel as if the water from the pool extended into the house.

To meet their desires, Franklin painted the walls and cabinets in similar hues. For interest, she used dark wood finish on the island, which grounded it to the middle of the room.

The designer then repeated the dark wood color throughout the rest of the house for continuity. She also used a light cream color inside the glass cabinets over the windows, which duplicated the countertop color and brightened the interiors of the cabinets. A frequent entertainer, the lady of the house wanted a range in the island so she could look out over the pool area while cooking. The graceful copper hood was the spot-on solution and balances the room perfectly.

The microwave is to the left of the refrigerator, with a drawer beneath it featuring a sliding shelf. Now the cook can pull open the drawer and have a landing place for a hot dish. As an added touch, forged acorn and branch hardware decorate the island. The final design was the perfect combination of function and style. «

DESIGNER
Mary Ann Cullens
Franklin, CKD
Designs by Five Inc.
4 S. Walnut St.
Statesboro, GA 30458
912.764.6020

SPECIAL FEATURES
Custom copper hood; custom color match on wall and base cabinets; stone mosaic tile backsplash; honed CaesarStone countertops; a large cook's island in rough knotty alder with 5-inch turned legs; corner lazy Susans; roll-out shelves

DIMENSIONS
16 x 16

PRODUCTS USED
Cabinetry: Geppetto Kitchens
Flooring: Casa Dolce Casa
Countertops: CaesarStone
Sink(s): Waternity
Faucets: Moen
Dishwasher: Bosch
Range: Wolf
Lighting: Recessed and undercabinet
Refrigerator: GE Profile
Wallcovering: Benjamin Moore Wythe Blue
Oven: GE Profile
Hood: Luxury Copper

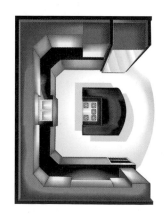

An Eye on Design

THE BIG CHALLENGE of this project was to create a kitchen space that would allow these young Vienna, Virginia, homeowners to keep an eye on the adjacent family room while in the kitchen. A stay-at-home mom, the lady of the house needed an accommodating design since she and the rest of the gang spend lot of time in the kitchen. And, at the same time the homeowners did not want to give up the traditional feel of the house by opening up the walls.

The homeowners called upon Marcelo Dobrauchi of Terranova Construction to come up with the ideal solution. Dobrauchi created an island to house the range, so that Mom can keep a close eye on the kids while they play nearby or talk to guests who are lounging in the adjacent family room. A bar-height counter on the island provides a space for family and guests to gather. Dobrauchi installed a beam on the ceiling to leave the room completely open, as a wall they removed was load bearing.

In order to maintain the traditional atmosphere of the house, Dobrauchi suggested dark, richly stained cabinets with the lighter toned countertop to create a little contrast. Also, using different heights on the cabinets gave this kitchen a more cozy, relaxed feel. «

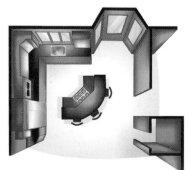

DESIGNER
Marcelo Dobrauchi
Terranova Construction,
K&B Inc.
8032 Leesburg Pike
Vienna, VA 22182
703.761.0604

SPECIAL FEATURES
Curved, multilevel
island; open floor plan

DIMENSIONS
26' x 22'

PRODUCTS USED
Cabinetry: Kraftmaid
Flooring: Hardwood
Countertops: Granite,
Santa Cecilia
Sink(s): Franke
Faucets: Grohe
Dishwasher: KitchenAid
Cooktop: GE Monogram
Lighting: Progress
Lighting pendants
Refrigerator: KitchenAid
Wallcovering: Behr paint

MEMBER OF
SEN DESIGN GROUP

Grand Openings

FAMILY TIME WAS important to these homeowners in Virginia. They wanted a new, bigger and functional kitchen, one that would merge seamlessly into the rest of the home and look as if it had always been there. An adjacent living room had been underused, and it was the homeowners' wish to blend that space with the kitchen. Marcelo Dobrauchi of Terranova Construction K&B was ready to transform their wishes into reality.

A small peninsula was the perfect design choice to marry the new kitchen space with the living room. The open floor plan helps showcase the central island for a striking visual effect and better flow and creates the illusion of a much larger home. The designers ensured continuity between the two spaces by extending the existing living room hardwood into the kitchen. The bi-color cabinetry gives the traditional-style kitchen a freshened-up feel. Also, different shades of Silestone for the countertops were used to create a nice contrast and a casual look.

For a focal point, the island was the natural choice. With its many functions—from cooking and prep to serving and eating—it's meant to represent the hearth of the kitchen. The open shelves on both ends, framed by posts, mimic a grand piece of furniture rather than a plain island. The final effect is an understated elegance with timeless cabinetry, a soothing color palette, interesting detail and very functional use of space. «

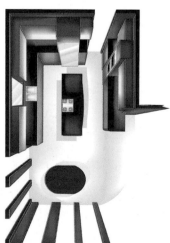

DESIGNER
Marcelo Dobrauchi
Terranova
Construction K&B
8032 Leesburg Pike
Vienna, VA 22182
703.761.0604

SPECIAL FEATURES
Multipurpose island; walk-in pantry; bi-color cabinets

DIMENSIONS
17 x 15

PRODUCTS USED
Cabinetry: Bertch Legacy, eggshell with brown glaze
Flooring: Hardwood
Countertops: Silestone Rosa Grey, field; Silestone mahogany, island
Sink(s): Blanco
Faucets: Danze
Dishwasher: GE
Cooktop: GE
Refrigerator: GE Profile
Oven: GE Profile
Lighting: Recessed

MEMBER OF
SEN DESIGN GROUP

PHOTOGRAPHER: JANE STANICH

Space for All

THIS HOME IN McAllen, Texas, built in 1967, was in need of a modern upgrade. The low ceiling, cramped space and lack of a pantry made this out-of-date kitchen in need of some major remodeling. To whip the kitchen into shape, the homeowners called upon Mary King of Signature Kitchens & Baths of McAllen.

The family does not entertain much, but they needed a design that allowed them to function comfortably and prepare delicious home-cooked meals. A large island serves as a beautiful focal point in the area, and also provides a place for the family to gather. It was important for the design team to create not only an accommodating area for the cook, but a relaxing area for the entire family. Now, Mom cooks while the kids sit comfortably doing homework and Dad finishes up his office work, all enjoying the newly remodeled space.

A pass-through from the kitchen to the dining room is highlighted by beautiful cabinets with glass door insets, accessible from both sides. The cabinetry also features glass shelving, which lets the light shine through and reflect off the colored glassware. «

DESIGNER
Mary King
Signature Kitchens &
Baths of McAllen
6500 N. 10th St., Ste. U
McAllen, TX 78504
956.213.8090

SPECIAL FEATURES
Island with seating for five

DIMENSIONS
17' x 17'

PRODUCTS USED
Cabinetry: Jay Rambo, clear alder wood, brown stone, Colonial
Flooring: Amtico, wood teak antique
Countertops: Granite, Copper Canyon
Sink(s): Blanco, stainless steel
Faucet: Pegasus, chrome
Dishwasher: KitchenAid
Cooktop: KitchenAid
Lighting: Task, belcaro pendants
Refrigerator: KitchenAid
Wallcovering: Daltile, La Costa Gold
Oven: KitchenAid

MEMBER OF
SEN DESIGN GROUP

PHOTOGRAPHER: JON KING KEISLING

Functional Elegance

THIS CONTEMPORARY KITCHEN in McAllen, Texas, was designed by Mary King of Signature Kitchen and Bath of McAllen with both form and function in mind. Because the homeowner loves to entertain and prepare gourmet meals, it was important that this kitchen was accommodating to her varying needs. The focal point is her large island, giving her plenty of area to prepare her special meals for her family and friends. This large kitchen gave her the ability to have an extensive appliance suite, as well as creative storage solutions.

To meet all her needs, the design team incorporated pullout cabinetry, a Magic Corner cabinet and a special cabinet for her Miele coffee machine. A KitchenAid double-drawer dishwasher ensures all the tableware will be clean at once, no matter what size the gathering! Pendant lighting gives the space a peaceful quality, illuminating the room beautifully.

To give the kitchen a unique appearance, the design team contrasted beautiful white Thermofoil cabinetry with an espresso quarter-sawn oak cabinetry on the island. Quartz countertops add another element of functional elegance. A custom nook area provides additional counter space next to her breakfast table. The kitchen is now her favorite part of her new home. «

DESIGNER
Mary King
Signature Kitchen and Bath of McAllen
6500 N. 10th St., Ste. U
McAllen, TX 78504
956.213.8090

SPECIAL FEATURES
Large custom island for prepping; mix of cabinet finishes

DIMENSIONS
13 x 20

PRODUCTS USED
Cabinetry: Jay Rambo, high-gloss white Thermofoil and espresso quarter-sawn oak
Countertops: Quartz
Dishwasher: KitchenAid
Cooktop: Wolf
Refrigerator: Sub-Zero
Oven: Wolf
Lighting: Task lighting, pendants

MEMBER OF
SEN DESIGN GROUP

PHOTOGRAPHER: DAVID PEZZAT

At Home in NYC

REGENCY DESIGNS' PRINCIPAL DESIGNER, Rochelle Kalisch, believes "the kitchen should be a space with an aura, full of personality and warmth." In every project Kalisch works to not only meet her client's expectations, but to exceed them. The kitchen in this New York City residence was no exception.

Owned by a couple who entertain occasionally, though not often, they wanted their kitchen to make efficient use of the existing space. They also desired a separate formal breakfast area. Kalisch was brought on board to oblige their requests.

Since the original layout did not include a window, the designer created large openings to allow natural light from other rooms to flood the kitchen. She also created three pantry cabinets complete with two archways. The archways exude a charming aesthetic and also assist in ushering light into the room. The middle pantry conceals a structural column. Since the kitchen is specifically created for meal prep and snacking, Kalisch also added a separate breakfast room. This area opens to the kitchen and allows the homeowners a proper place to gather for meals. A window over the sink provides a view into the entryway, and light-hued cherry cabinets enhance the overall design. The result is a space that exudes a sense of warmth, a culinary creation that meets and exceeds the homeowners' desires. «

DESIGNER
Rochelle Kalisch
Regency Designs Inc.
204 E. 77 St., Apt. 1-E
New York, NY 10021
212.517.8707

SPECIAL FEATURES
Special pantry cabinets to hide metal pole; glass pantries with archways between kitchen and dinette; island attached to pantry on one side

DIMENSIONS
14 x 16

PRODUCTS USED
Cabinetry: Acorn Kitchens
Countertops: Granite
Sink(s): Franke
Dishwasher: KitchenAid
Cooktop: Dacor, Gaggenau
Refrigerator: KitchenAid
Oven: Dacor
Warming Drawer: Dacor

MEMBER OF
SEN DESIGN GROUP

PHOTOGRAPHER: ALISON HAHN

Bungalow Style

WITH A CIRCA-1950S KITCHEN IN DIRE NEED of a major overhaul, these Colorado homeowners wanted a culinary creation that would incorporate all the perks of 21st-century design into their vintage bungalow. Though they have no children and rarely entertain, the couple still wanted a comfortable place that would feel welcoming and would integrate their individual needs with their personal style. With these objectives in mind, the owners targeted Judy Pepper of Pepper Design Associates Inc. to spice up their space.

Not surprisingly, the decades-old kitchen lacked storage and counter space, so Pepper promptly set about transforming the room into an open layout with ample places to stow their stuff. After gutting the room, she added a series of storage, chopping and prep/baking/cooking centers to meet the couple's functional needs.

Because the clients are enamored of arches, Pepper arched the kitchen shutters. She also removed the existing 8-foot ceiling and created a new one that reaches 17 feet at its highest point. An in-floor heating system keeps the room toasty in winter. Other noteworthy elements include a farmhouse sink, a dishwasher with drawers and a large pantry. Not only did the owners get the kitchen of their dreams, but they also got more: an expansive space that typifies a modern kitchen while retaining the flavor of a bygone era. «

DESIGNER
Judy Pepper
Pepper Design
Associates Inc.
11540 W. 84th Place
Arvada, CO 80005
303.424.8404

SPECIAL FEATURES
Slab-granite 18-inch-high backsplash; multilevel island; chiseled-granite edge detail; undermount sinks; air switch for garbage disposal

DIMENSIONS
31 x 25

PRODUCTS USED
Sink(s): Bates veggie sink
Refrigerator: GE counter-depth refrigerator and refrigerated drawers
Oven: GE Advantium
Dishwasher: KitchenAid

MEMBER OF
SEN DESIGN GROUP

One of a Kind

Undivided attention was given to each detail in this Longboat Key condo's kitchen, as the homeowners and the designer, Michael O'Connor of Signature Kitchens and Baths of Sarasota, joined together to create a space that would eventually raise the standard in kitchen design.

The elements in the kitchen seem to come alive as they integrate seamlessly with one another. The grain of the custom cabinets' exotic veneer solicits a "wow" from anyone who sees the kitchen. Matching the cabinetry is a soffit that mirrors the shape of the striking granite below, enhancing the flow of the entire space. Stainless steel, glass, and porcelain tile combine in a backsplash so stunning they seem to sing in harmony.

Throughout the kitchen, hidden storage solutions facilitate the homeowners' daily activities. A 48-inch pantry houses pull-out systems for nonperishables. Large drawers are outfitted to house plates, serving pieces, and cookware, and curved tall cabinets are designed to hold cleaning equipment. Behind the pocketing doors of the 36-inch pantry lies a breakfast bar complete with countertop, coffee maker, toaster oven, and drawers for everyday use.

Upon completion of the project, the homeowners raised their glasses of champagne to the designer and construction crew in recognition of raising the standard in kitchen design. «

DESIGNER
Michael O' Connor
Signature Kitchens and
Baths of Sarasota
6528 S. Tamiami Trail
Sarasota, FL 34231
941.894.6692

SPECIAL FEATURES
Book-matched exotic veneer, bi-directional roll-out drawers in island, custom pull-out pantries, undercabinet electrical strips, butler's pantry, recessed cubby over cooktop, intricate lighting package, peg-board organization systems in all drawers

DIMENSIONS
12 x 13, 5 x 7

PRODUCTS USED
Cabinetry: In-house Custom Cabinetry
Flooring: 18 x 18 Elemente Terra tile set in brick pattern
Countertops: Capolavoro granite
Sink(s): Houzer stainless steel
Faucets: Danze pull-down; Franke Little Butler
Refrigerator: KitchenAid built-in with custom panels
Cooktop: KitchenAid
Oven: KitchenAid
Dishwasher: KitchenAid two-drawer
Wine Cooler: KitchenAid
Lighting: Hunter Geometry
Wallcovering: Oxido porcelain, Jasba stainless steel, Bel Sol glass
Hardware: Dekkor

MEMBER OF
SEN DESIGN GROUP

PHOTOGRAPHER: GENE POLLUX

Old Is New Again

AFTER LIVING IN their residence for 30 years, these homeowners were ready for a big change. The abode's most dramatic transformation: the kitchen and dining area, which Jillaine Burton of Callen Construction took from a small, utilitarian space to a large, open gathering area.

To create a spacious and lofty feel, two large load-bearing walls were removed and a sun porch was absorbed into the main space. Burton then added a large, nearly circular island, which became the focal point of the design. The multitasking piece integrates prep space, cooking, and cleanup, with secondary cooking and refrigeration on the periphery.

The necessary support columns were added into the island layout, helping create a strong—but not overpowering—focal point. To create visual depth, light-colored cabinetry was set against the room's spicy colors and dramatic granite countertops. Marmoleum was the flooring of choice, blending with the many color palettes throughout open design.

An interesting challenge was to embellish the ceiling in the dining area, which was designed to look like a tray ceiling. Crown molding, rope lighting, and a warm uplit ambiance each add to the illusion of a larger space. With its fresh face and functional features, this reinvented space is sure to play host to large gatherings and small get-togethers for decades to come. «

DESIGNER
Jillaine Burton
Callen Construction
S63 W13131 Janesville Road
Muskego, WI 53150
414.529.5509

SPECIAL FEATURES
Circular-style working island

DIMENSIONS
14 x 28

PRODUCTS USED
Cabinetry: StarMark in Maple Honey with chocolate glaze
Flooring: Forbo Marmoleum
Countertops: Misk granite
Sink(s): Kohler
Faucet: Kohler Vinnata
Refrigerator: Sub-Zero
Cooktop: Electrolux
Oven: Viking
Warming Drawer: Wolf
Dishwasher: ASKO
Lighting: Kichler
Downdraft: Best by Broan

MEMBER OF
SEN DESIGN GROUP

PHOTOGRAPHER: MARK HEFFRON

Pinnacle of Design

THE OWNERS OF THIS Tampa Bay, Florida, home knew just what they wanted their kitchen to look like. To actualize their desires, they called on the team of Christine and Jim Macholz of Spotlight Kitchen & Bath Galleria, who shared their vision of a warm and inviting space with Old World charm.

The integrated appliances blend seamlessly with the rest of the cabinetry, just as the overall kitchen design melds effortlessly with the home. Stacked Dutch Made cabinetry draws the eye to the peak of the cathedral ceilings, with soft cream-colored raised-panel doors and a classic beaded inset frame.

Magnificent molding, flutes, columns, pilasters, keys and corbels are just a few of the many design features of this kitchen. A smaller prep island with a soapstone countertop is on wheels, easily rolled into the formal dining room. One large multilevel island—painted black for contrast—has a beautifully carved stone farm sink, appliances and a large seating area.

The butler's pantry has plenty of cabinets, an area for wine storage, refrigeration, a small bar sink, coffee machine and prep area for entertaining. A library ladder allows the homeowners to reach even the highest cabinets. When it was completed, the homeowners were delighted to see their vision brought to reality. «

DESIGNER
Christine Macholz
Spotlight Kitchen
& Bath Galleria
1183 Cedar St.
Safety Harbor, FL 34695
727.712.0029

SPECIAL FEATURES
Multi-stacked cabinets
with flutes and pilasters;
top cabinets show
glass and mullions; two
islands, one multilevel,
the other a "movable"
smaller island with
soapstone countertop

DIMENSIONS
25 x 18

PRODUCTS USED
Cabinetry: Dutch Made
Cabinetry, maple,
painted-glazed
Flooring: Dal-Tile,
porcelain tiles
Countertops: Dal-Tile,
Golden Persa and
Black Galaxy granite,
soapstone
Sink(s): Stone Forest,
granite farm sink;
copper bar sink
Faucets: Danze
Dishwasher: Bosch
Cooktop: Thermador
Oven: Thermador
Refrigerator: Thermador
Coffee machine: Miele
Hardware: Top Knobs
Hood: Eldorado Stone
Backsplash: Dal-tile;
design by Chris Macholz

MEMBER OF
SEN DESIGN GROUP

Maximizing Marvel

WHEN THE OWNERS of this Oldsmar, Fla., home decided to remodel, they called on the husband and wife team of Christine and Jim Macholz, designers and owners of Spotlight Kitchen & Bath Galleria, and Jamco Unlimited Inc., a contracting firm. They were given the task of maximizing space, changing the flow of traffic and designing a warm and inviting kitchen that opens to the living area.

The team designed a large island, which acts as a serving and prepping area, as well as a gathering spot for friends and family. Cabinets in front of the island allow for extra storage. The tile floor was replaced with walnut wood floors, and beautiful crown moulding is installed on the walls throughout the home, which adds warmth and flow.

A wine niche designed especially for the husband—lovingly named "The Wall of Anthony" by his wife—displays beautiful glasses and houses special wines from across the world. Coordinating custom cabinetry furthers the room's aesthetics and allows the appliances to seamlessly blend without sacrificing style.

A custom backsplash and Golden Typhoon granite countertops accentuate the room and are well lit by Tiffany pendants that were matched with a Tiffany chandelier—a beloved family heirloom. The final outcome is a spacious kitchen that boasts functionality and features various touches of the clients' personality throughout. «

DESIGNER

Christine Macholz CKBR
Spotlight Kitchen & Bath Galleria
1183 Cedar St.
Safety Harbor, FL 34695
727.712.0029

SPECIAL FEATURES
Tumbled stone and metal medallion featured on two walls; corbels beneath hood and corners of island

DIMENSIONS
25 X 27

PRODUCTS USED
Cabinetry: Holiday Kitchens
Flooring: City Plank Brazilian walnut
Countertops: Granite
Sink(s): Artisan
Faucet(s): Danze
Dishwasher: GE Profile
Cooktop: GE Profile
Lighting: Task
Refrigerator: GE Profile
Wallcovering: Tumbled stone, Vallarta and Questech metals
Oven: GE Profile
Microwave: GE Profile

MEMBER OF
SEN DESIGN GROUP

Clad in Class

AFTER BUILDING MANY new kitchens for customers, the owners of Bel Air Construction, Michael and Terri Watts, decided to remodel their own. The Watts' home is often the hub of family and friend gatherings, and the existing kitchen had limited space for guests, cooking and serving. The high degree of structural complexity set initial challenges, all of which were magnificently overcome to produce this stately space.

As avid entertainers, the Watts' found their primary goal was to create a spacious room to make hosting their frequent guests comfortable and convenient. Clad in state-of-the-art appliances, this open design makes entertaining exciting, and the massive windows provide an extravagant view. A large island serves multiple purposes, including the location for a convenient pop-up outlet strip to accommodate the room's luxury features.

To create a warm ambiance, the homeowners selected furniture-style wood front cabinetry to conceal the appliances. The warmth is furthered by the breathtaking view and natural light, displayed in the enormous windows. The combination of materials, stunning colors, and design make this kitchen welcoming to the large groups who visit their home. In the end, the homeowners were able to fulfill their needs while creating a design masterpiece. «

DESIGNER
Michael Watts CGR
Bel Air Construction Inc.
1655 Robin Circle
Forest Hill, MD 21050
410.557.9838

SPECIAL FEATURES
Oversized island with many appliances

DIMENSIONS
24 X 25

PRODUCTS USED
Cabinetry: Dura Supreme
Flooring: American Olean
Countertops: Granite
Sink(s): Blanco
Faucet(s): Brizo
Dishwasher: KitchenAid
Cooktop: KitchenAid
Lighting: Kichler
Refrigerator: KitchenAid
Backsplash: Daltile
Ovens: KitchenAid
Microwave: Sharp
Warming drawer: KitchenAid
Pot filler: Jaclo

MEMBER OF
SEN DESIGN GROUP

Fit for a Family

THE HOMEOWNERS OF this new home in Georgia had specific requirements for their kitchen. For starters, they needed several workstations, so multiple cooks could work and multiple tasks could be accomplished at the same time. To ensure the design worked for this large family, Jim Meloy, CKD, of Kitchen and Bath Concepts tailored the design to meet the family's lifestyle.

To give the cook easy access to all the primary zones of the home, Meloy separated the workstations. Convenient to the cooking center, the island incorporates a variety of storage solutions plus integrated refrigerator drawers and a prep sink. The microwave and warming drawer are a few steps away in the raised bar area. A generous pantry was pivotal to accommodating the food storage needs.

Meloy used distressed pine cabinets on the island, the raised bar, and a desk area, which contrasts with the weathered butter cream cabinetry of the rest of the kitchen. The brown motif repeats itself in the copper farmhouse sink, oil-rubbed bronze faucets, and hardware. The slate floor is great for the high traffic of pets and children, and the desk is set discreetly out of the way of the hustle and bustle. A custom table for 12 to 14 sits in the adjoining informal dining area, which is perfect for this family's entertaining. «

DESIGNER
Jim Meloy, CKD
Kitchen and Bath
Concepts
11444 Alpharetta Hwy.
Roswell, GA 30076
770.442.9845

SPECIAL FEATURES
Multiwork zones for large family, walk-in pantry behind doors that match cabinets, complementary to adjacent rooms

DIMENSIONS
13 x 27

PRODUCTS USED
Cabinetry: Wayne Co.
Flooring: Slate
Countertops: St. Cecelia granite
Sinks: De la Frontera
Faucets: Rohl
Refrigerator: Sub-Zero
Cooktop: Wolf
Oven: Wolf
Dishwasher: Fisher & Paykel
Other: Pedal Valve

MEMBER OF
SEN DESIGN GROUP

PHOTOGRAPHER: JOHN UMBERGER

Asian Aesthetic

THE OWNERS OF AN ARTS AND CRAFTS-STYLE HOME had a specific vision of how they wanted their kitchen to look. They wanted clean, modern lines as well as elements reflective of their Asian heritage; they also wanted to keep the overall aesthetic very balanced. To achieve this goal, the couple hired Zachary Simmons and Chris Elkins of CKS to create a stunning kitchen.

The designers began by installing a large center island. The custom-made zebra wood table fulfilled the owners' desire for guest seating. The designers also added a larger work space, a preparation sink and a butcher-block insert. To facilitate the open flow and movement for which Asian design is so well known, the designers removed the wall in front of the main sink to provide a view of the adjoining family room. To create a focal point that can be seen from the family room, the design team created an expansive walnut frame with metal veneer, highlighting the entire wall behind the range. They also concealed the once-visible pantry door by replacing it with rift-cut oak paneling. The designers created innovative space solutions by incorporating a pull-out countertop hidden in the wall below the coffee maker and dish drawers with adjustable wooden pegs that allow dishes to be stored next to the dishwasher.

The result of this total transformation is a kitchen that reflects the owners' needs for organization and a sense of personal style. «

DESIGNERS
Chris Elkins,
Zack Simmons
CKS
2408 Reichard St.
Durham, NC 27705
919.477.6318

SPECIAL FEATURES
Book-matched rift-cut oak panels used on perimeter walls; zebra wood table resting on sea-foam green granite-covered island, end-cut butcher block

DIMENSIONS
16 × 17

PRODUCTS USED
Cabinetry: Custom by CKS
Flooring: Byrd tile
Countertops: Sea-foam green granite; zebra wood; end-cut butcher block
Sink: Oliveri
Faucets: Hansgrohe
Dishwasher: Miele
Cooktop: Wolf
Lighting: Monorail, Murano Blue, LBL Fusion
Refrigerator: Sub-Zero
Wallcovering: Nu Metal
Wine cooler: Sub-Zero
Coffee maker: Miele

MEMBER OF
SEN DESIGN GROUP

Historically Home

IT WAS AN incredible project from the beginning when Lisa Principe of CKS Design Studio was selected along with New York-based designer Seborn Ragsdale of Seborn Ragsdale Interiors to essentially gut and remodel this family estate home, originally built in the 1800s. The primary goal for this home was to create a room comfortable for a large family with small children, while concurrently retaining the historical elements in the rest of the house.

The kitchen was made more functional by removing an adjoining wall to add space for the two islands and breakfast nook. Seating is incorporated in both islands, at different heights, to accommodate children and adults. To increase the convenience of preparation and cleanup, modern stainless appliances, multiple sinks and dishwashers accommodate large meals and entertaining.

The perimeter features white painted inset cabinetry with period hardware, beadboard, turnings and clover leaf punched steel inserts. For contrast, the islands are finished in a silvery blue-green paint, and a quarter-sawn oak desk and hutch are stained in a rich dark-cocoa brown. Perimeter countertops, created in cherry plank, are stained to coordinate with the beams and paneling at the ceiling. The finished project is incredible, suiting family and designer alike. «

DESIGNER
Lisa Principe
CKS Design Studio
2408 Reichard St.
Durham, NC 27705
919.477.6318

Seborn Ragsdale
Seborn Ragsdale
Interiors
1133 Broadway, Ste. 702
New York, NY 10010
214.741.1435

SPECIAL FEATURES
Painted cabinetry
with period hardware;
custom hutch; large
wooden beams and
tongue and groove
paneling

DIMENSIONS
34 x 20

PRODUCTS USED
Cabinetry: Dura
Supreme
Cabinet hardware: Van
Dyke's Restorers, Top
Knobs, Berenson
Countertops: Signature
Custom Woodworking,
Schneider Stone
Sink(s): Rohl, Kohler
Faucet(s): Danze
Dishwasher: Bosch
Range: Wolf
Hood: Wolf
Wine chiller: Marvel
Ice maker: Sub-Zero
Wall oven: Dacor
Microwave: Dacor
Warming drawer: Dacor
Refrigerator: Sub-Zero
Wallcovering: Ann Sacks
Panels: Barker Metalcraft
Pot filler: Danze

MEMBER OF
SEN DESIGN GROUP

PHOTOGRAPHER: MICHAEL TRAISTER

Deliciously Detailed

THIS KEYSTONE, COLORADO, kitchen combines luscious chocolate, caramel, and cream colors with inviting curves and varying cabinet heights to make this large room deliciously delightful. Linda Miller, Allied ASID, of Aspen Grove Kitchen & Bath, Inc., incorporated a curved slab granite bar top on the island, mirroring the curves found in the structural beams overhead. The curve is repeated once again in the front of the hammered-copper apron-front sink.

Miller worked with the owners of this second home to create a kitchen layout that allows the person cooking to still visit with family and guests, most notably by placing the cooktop in the island. The island also houses a bar sink and wine cooler on one side, so the owners can access it conveniently when entertaining without having to move into the main work area.

Utilizing cabinets in different colors, Miller was able to fill the oversized space with interesting and creative storage for the owners' cookware and collectables. Perhaps the crown jewel of the space, a furniture-style hutch was created to serve as a focal point for those entering the kitchen. This unique piece is decorative as well as functional, as it contains and displays the owners' collection of beautiful pottery-style dishes. «

DESIGNER
Linda G. Miller, Allied ASID
Aspen Grove Kitchen & Bath, Inc.
721 Granite, A1
Frisco, CO 80443
970.468.5393

SPECIAL FEATURES
Two-level island with curved bar top, decorative travertine tile finish on back of island, hutch-style furniture piece as a focal point

DIMENSIONS
14 x 19

PRODUCTS USED
Cabinetry: Medallion Cabinetry Designer series
Flooring: Natural sandstone
Countertops: Slab granite
Sink(s): Hammered copper
Refrigerator: KitchenAid
Cooktop: Wolf
Oven: KitchenAid
Dishwasher: Bosch

MEMBER OF
SEN DESIGN GROUP

PHOTOGRAPHER: STEVEN PAUL WHITSITT

The Right Angles

THE BIGGEST CHALLENGE in this Mills River, North Carolina, home was working around the timbers in the peg frame. The design team led by April Hand of Benbow & Associates Inc. was ready to tackle the task head-on and deliver a functional design.

A lot of planning went into the height of the wall cabinetry, as well as the number of cabinets to be included in the design. It had to be the perfect amount to ensure the timbers weren't hidden or overwhelmed. The team placed the island between two of the timbers in the center of the room, making sure each cabinet fit around the other timbers along the perimeter walls. They also designed the base cabinets to sit in front of the timbers.

The knobs on all cabinets are one-of-a-kind solid Vermont soapstone, adding a true touch of personality. Custom-made shelves and corbels by Benbow & Associates provide another facet of panache. The tumbled slate backsplash with integrated glass tiles is a perfect focal point. And since these homeowners enjoy entertaining, the designers included a small bar area off to the side of the kitchen. This new spot to enjoy a cocktail is the perfect locale for the homeowners to admire their new epicurean space. «

DESIGNER
April Hand
Benbow & Associates Inc.
38 Glendale Ave.
Ashville, NC 28803
828.281.2700

SPECIAL FEATURES
Handmade glass tile backsplash, solid Vermont soapstone knobs

DIMENSIONS
20 x 11

PRODUCTS USED
Cabinetry: Medallion
Flooring: Cut rock
Countertops: Cambria
Sink(s): KitchenAid
Faucets: Kohler
Refrigerator: KitchenAid
Cooktop: KitchenAid
Oven: KitchenAid
Dishwasher: KitchenAid

MEMBER OF
SEN DESIGN GROUP

PHOTOGRAPHER: DAVID DETRICK

Sleek Stylings

THIS NEW KITCHEN in Asheville, North Carolina, needed to be custom-designed to fit this small family. The design team of Benbow & Associates worked closely with the builder, Nancy Padgett of High Country Builders, and homeowners Karen and Steve Blair to create a sleek, contemporary kitchen, loaded with accessories and special features.

For starters, universal toe kicks in stainless steel were incorporated throughout the kitchen, providing perfect harmony with the stainless steel sink. Concrete countertops make a bold statement and glass tile accents give an extra splash of flair. The Cumaru flooring adds a warm and beautifully dynamic touch to the room.

They say that design is in the details, and this kitchen is truly no exception. Tray dividers in the smooth-gliding Blumotion drawers make everything simple to find. A spice drawer and a rollout tray further supplement the organization factor. Trash pullouts keep waste bins discreet until ready for use, and the deep storage drawers hold even the biggest pots and pans with ease. The microwave drawer is another element of within-reach design, making warming up foods quick and easy.

In the end, the design was a perfect combination of sleek, high-end design and family-functional features. «

DESIGNER
Jennifer Barker
Benbow & Associates Inc.
38 Glendale Ave.
Asheville, NC 28803
828.281.2700

SPECIAL FEATURES
Increased-height cabinetry with countertops at 38 inches; increased-height stainless steel toe kick; Blumotion glides and concrete countertops

DIMENSIONS
14 x 16

PRODUCTS USED
Cabinetry: Frameless cherry
Flooring: Cumaru, Southern chestnut
Countertops: Concrete
Sink(s): Blanco, stainless steel, prep; Blanco, main
Faucets: Dornbracht
Dishwasher: Miele
Cooktop: Wolf
Refrigerator: Samsung
Wallcovering: Paint and tile
Oven: Miele
Microwave drawer: Sharp
Vent hood: Zephyr
Hardware: Top Knobs

MEMBER OF
SEN DESIGN GROUP

PHOTOGRAPHER: DAVID DIETRICH

Room with a View

THE OWNERS OF THIS DWELLING, overlooking downtown Asheville, N.C., wanted to create a kitchen that more closely blended with the style of their house. Their children grown, the couple also desired a culinary space where they could cook mouthwatering meals while reveling in the unrivaled view of their city. To help realize their dreams, the homeowners brought Jennifer K. Barker of Benbow & Associates on board to tackle the many-tiered remodel project.

Throughout the design and selection process, Barker worked closely with the homeowners. They chose German antique glass and glass shelving to add an Old World touch and added wood panels to the existing black-paneled refrigerator to create a built-in look. Notable features include the beaded inset construction with a mixture of door styles, tumbled slate tile accents and a functional cabinetry layout.

Incorporating the existing butler's pantry with the new design was the biggest sticking point. To overcome the challenge, Barker and the homeowners set the floor tiles at a diagonal and chose a paint color to unify the two rooms. Slate tile in the kitchen meshes with the gray tones of the granite in the pantry and pulls together the warm tones in the kitchen. Thanks to the team effort, this room with a view sports an uptown look that's on par with the rest of the home. «

DESIGNER
Jennifer K. Barker
Benbow & Associates
38 Glendale Ave.
Asheville, NC 28803
828.281.2700

SPECIAL FEATURES
German antique glass; custom mantel piece; bump-outs; single-height island counter; layered mouldings; tumbled slate tiles

DIMENSIONS
13 x 18

PRODUCTS USED
Cabinetry: Benbow & Associates Blue Ridge Collection
Flooring: Tile
Countertops: Peacock Gold Granite
Sink(s): Franke
Faucets: Delta
Dishwasher: Bosch
Range: Dacor
Warming drawer: Dacor
Refrigerator: GE Monogram
Wallcovering: Paint, tile
Oven: Dacor warming oven
Microwave: Sharp microwave drawer
Hardware: Schaub

MEMBER OF
SEN DESIGN GROUP

PHOTOGRAPHER: DAVID DIETR CH

Seaside Serenity

WHEN THE OWNERS of this West Harwich, Mass., weekend home decided to build their house, they didn't want to take any chances with the design of their kitchen. Wanting an aesthetic that reflected their lifestyle, the clients aimed to combine their love of fine living, entertaining and the surrounding beach environment. After researching, they hired Mariette Barsoum of Divine Kitchens to bring their vision of a cottage kitchen to life.

Prevo cabinetry sets the stage with crisp white reverse raised-panel doors and classic beaded inset frame. The integrated refrigeration, warming drawer and dishwasher are paneled and blend seamlessly with the rest of the cabinetry. Stacked cabinets attract the eye to the peak of the cathedral ceiling. The elegant mantel hood, adorned with corbels, creates a fabulous focal point above the five-burner gas cooktop. Crown molding and oil-rubbed bronze hardware and fixtures add elegant detail. Seeded glass fronts mimic the pebbles found outside the door. The backsplash is designed in soft, sand-colored tiles, adding interest without calling too much attention to it. In the end, the comfortable beach house provides all the necessities of fine living. «

DESIGNER
Mariette Barsoum
Divine Kitchens LLC
40 Lyman St.
Westborough, MA 01581
508.366.5670

SPECIAL FEATURES
Stacked cabinets with seeded glass fronts on upper half; beadboard paneled island; paneled integrated appliances

DIMENSIONS
15 x 13.5

PRODUCTS USED
Cabinetry: Prevo
Countertops: Absolute Black honed granite
Dishwasher: Bosch
Cooktop: Wolf
Refrigerator: Sub-Zero
Oven: Wolf
Refrigerator drawers: Sub-Zero
Warming drawer: Wolf
Hood: Best

MEMBER OF
SEN DESIGN GROUP

PHOTOGRAPHER: LORETTA BERARDINELLI

Artistic Flair

FOR THEIR CONTEMPORARY renovation in this
Framingham, Mass., home these homeowners enlisted
Mariette Barsoum CKD of Divine Kitchens. Though the
homeowners desired ample storage, they also wished to
create an open flow that would be conducive to entertaining.
With the owners' design interests in mind, Barsoum
endeavored to improve the practicality of the kitchen while
adding an artistic flair.

The slab maple cabinetry with large stainless steel pulls
acts as the kitchen's primary contemporary element. Adding
curves in the corner wall cabinet, Barsoum mimicked
the design element with the shape of the granite island.
To further rid the kitchen of straight lines, she designed
multiple levels in the cabinetry and in the island.

Contrasting the circular feel of the rest of the kitchen,
the backsplash, hardware and barstools share an artistic
square motif. For added interest, Barsoum
combined materials such as granite and
Corian countertops and ceramic tile and
bamboo floors. To increase the artistic
flair, the homeowners chose cobalt blue
light fixtures and accessories, making their
kitchen a visually stimulating place to dine
and entertain. «

DESIGNER
Mariette Barsoum
Divine Kitchens LLC
40 Lyman St.
Westborough, MA 01581
508.336.5670

SPECIAL FEATURES
Curved, open-corner
wall cabinet; lift-up
cabinet doors: two-level
bar seats

DIMENSIONS
15 x 24

PRODUCTS USED
Cabinetry: Divine
Kitchens
Flooring: Ceramic tile,
bamboo wood
Countertops: Granite
(island); Corian (on
perimeter)
Cooktop: Wolf
Refrigerator: Kenmore
Oven: Jenn-Air
Wine Refrigerator:
Vinotemp
Microwave: GE Profile

MEMBER OF
SEN DESIGN GROUP

PHOTOGRAPHER: LORETTA BERARDINELLI

Modern Cucina

SITUATED IN ORANGE, CALIFORNIA, this 40-year-old home features a 6-by-12-foot U-shaped kitchen. The homeowners, however, desired an open, spacious area conducive to entertaining. To create their dream design, they called on Candice Winer of Quality Kitchens Direct.

Since the kitchen remodel posed a challenge that plagues many Southern Californians—though the value of the home warranted a large kitchen, ample space was an obstacle—Winer combined the kitchen and adjacent dining room to create a "great room." Her goal: to create separate food prep and cleanup areas designed to make the kitchen as efficient as possible. Winer maximized the space by installing a central island. With its contrasting colors, diverse door style and vast spindle legs designed to replicate the look of furniture, the island is the room's focal point. A centrally located sink further enables the chef to engage with guests while preparing food.

In addition to its functional benefits, the kitchen also boasts beautiful elements. Installed in a grid pattern, the floor anchors the room and creates a visual flow between the kitchen and the living room, which makes the house appear larger. The finished cucina is now the heart of the family's home. «

DESIGNER
Candice Winer
Quality Kitchens Direct
1938 N. Batavia St.
Suite F
Orange, CA 92865
714.997.4789

SPECIAL FEATURES
Split-face travertine backsplash with custom mosaic; distressed, glazed, hand-rubbed through finish; wood with travertine insert flooring

DIMENSIONS
20 x 12

PRODUCTS USED
Cabinetry: Dura Supreme
Flooring: Hand distressed with travertine insert
Countertops: Granite
Sinks: Blanco
Faucet(s): Waterstone
Dishwasher: Fisher & Paykel
Cooktop: Thermador
Refrigerator: Jenn-Air
Oven: Thermador Pro

Mountain Getaway

THIS KITCHEN IS in a new home located in Silverstone, Colorado. The builder, Vasiliy Gantsyak of D.I.A.N.A. Service Inc., beautifully blended his love of the mountains with his Ukrainian background. Working with Amanda Good at Aspen Grove Kitchen and Bath, he was able to bring mountain elegance to the kitchen design.

One of the challenges was to create enough cabinet storage in a small space while maintaining plenty of visual interest. The team, however, overcame this obstacle in spades. The two colors in the kitchen, as well as multilevel cabinets, make for a stunning visual impact. And the slate and red oak flooring are the perfect complement to the granite countertops. No detail was overlooked, and the design is as functional as it is beautiful. Plenty of storage throughout the space keeps everything organized and easy to find.

The attention to detail is evident in every nook and cranny in this nature-inspired space. The beautiful mountain vistas are mirrored in the tile backsplash, as well as in the stone over the vent hood. The rough-edged, free-form island is a lovely contrast to the sleek stainless steel appliances. The tile accents used on the wall are a stunning addition. The builder's careful distressing found throughout the house is mirrored in the kitchen cabinets as well. No luxury is sacrificed in this picture-perfect Rocky Mountain getaway. «

DESIGNER
Amanda Good
Aspen Grove Kitchen
and Bath
Frisco, CO 80442
970.468.5393

Vasiliy Gantsyak
D.I.A.N.A. Service Inc.
970.389.2931

SPECIAL FEATURES
Free-form island;
multilevel cabinets

DIMENSIONS
10 x 13

PRODUCTS USED
Cabinetry: Medallion Designer, Alder with Carriage Black and Harvest Bronze
Flooring: Slate with red oak
Countertops: Granite
Sink(s): Kohler
Faucets: Delta
Dishwasher: Jenn-Air
Refrigerator: Jenn-Air
Wallcovering: Faux paint with tile
Oven: Jenn-Air

MEMBER OF
SEN DESIGN GROUP

PHOTOGRAPHER: TIMOTHY FAUST

Simple Comfort

An outmoded 1960s home in Palo Alto, California, this once-drab dwelling needed a facelift both in terms of function and design. The existing kitchen was too walled-in and forced an awkward traffic flow through the space when friends and family wanted to access the popular outdoor pool area.

Michael Sullivan of Norwell Design Build began with a fresh look for the overall floor plan of the home. The solution included the relocation of the main entry and stairs, enabling the kitchen to expand and open up to the adjacent living areas. Changing the placement of the kitchen and breakfast area improved the flow of traffic, and the new open floor plan provides a more social and entertainment-friendly atmosphere for a busy household.

A seismic upgrade of the entire home, which stands directly on the San Andreas Fault, afforded the opportunity to install traditional timber framing throughout the home—imparting warmth, charm and a sense of history. Rustic cherry cabinets and distressed, black-painted island cabinets combine to reinforce the new lived-in feel of the home, along with reclaimed French terra-cotta floor pavers and hand-scraped, wide-plank, hickory flooring.

Stunning in style and substance, this new country kitchen became the inspiration for a complete home remodel that better suits its owner's lifestyle. «

DESIGNER
Michael Sullivan NKBA
Norwell Design Build
2250 Park Blvd.
Palo Alto, CA 94306

SPECIAL FEATURES
Hand-hewn post and beam construction; hand-scraped hickory plank floor; reclaimed French terra-cotta pavers; cherry butcher block island; custom-painted pictorial backsplash tile

DIMENSIONS
24' x 12'

PRODUCTS USED
Cabinetry: Crystal
Flooring: Homerwood hickory, hand-scraped
Countertops: Cherry butcher block; granite
Sink(s): Rohl
Dishwasher: Bosch
Range: GE Monogram

PHOTOGRAPHER: JIM WRIGHT

California Cucina

OWNED BY A SINGLE WOMAN, this California townhouse was in need of a complete overhaul. To accomplish the task, the homeowner called on Norwell Design/Build of Palo Alto. Norwell began the project by gutting the home, which also included substantial structural work. The biggest challenge: working around tight spaces and an outdated, closed-in design between rooms. To bring its client's dream kitchen to life, Norwell removed the wall between the dining area and the existing U-shaped kitchen. This helped to open the area. The removal of the wall also allowed natural light from the adjacent room to flood the kitchen, and it further created a space conducive to entertaining.

Norwell incorporated a variety of special design features within the room. Hardwood flooring and mouldings throughout the first floor tie each individual space together. A travertine tile backsplash serves as a focal point in the kitchen. Norwell also opted to utilize this same travertine on the fireplace surround, which they applied in a large pattern simulating block construction. Additional backsplash tiles situated above the travertine and a pendant light hanging over the sink add focus and ambiance to a wall sans window. A custom island with beadboard paneling and furniture corbels, vintage schoolhouse light fixtures and a custom panel refrigerator top off this space. «

DESIGNER
Ian Wheeler
Norwell Design/Build
2248 Park Blvd.
Palo Alto, CA 94306
650.323.1142

SPECIAL FEATURES
Custom island with beadboard paneling, furniture corbels; vintage schoolhouse light fixtures; custom panel refrigerator

DIMENSIONS
9 x 13

PRODUCTS USED
Cabinetry: Custom
Flooring: Quarter-sawn white oak
Countertops: Uba Tuba granite
Sink(s): Franke stainless undermount
Faucet(s): Rohl
Dishwasher: Bosch
Range: GE
Lighting: Vintage Schoolhouse
Refrigerator: Jenn-Air
Backsplash: Honed Beaumaniere travertine, French limestone mouldings, pewter accents

PHOTOGRAPHER: JIM WRIGHT

Perfect Triangle

THE LARGE EXPANSE of space in this kitchen challenged the ability to place appliances and work centers at a practical and functional proximity to each other. To accommodate all the requirements of the space, Vicki Edwards of Kitchen & Bath Images set to work.

The large island helped to balance function and practicality. Two standard size sinks were placed at the window for clean-up. Another one on the island functioned as a prep sink. The raised portion of the island provided a place to position the microwave, which now sits directly across from the refrigerator and close to the prep area.

The next challenges were to fit the kitchen cabinets to the scale of the space, and to implement a style that complimented the Italianate-themed home. That was achieved by taking cabinets to a much taller height than normal, and double stacking doors to give a more substantial and proportioned relationship to the 12-foot ceilings. A counter-height table was positioned on the backside of the island for casual dining.

A butler's pantry opened to the kitchen and connected the space to a hallway that led to the dining room. The cabinets were a breathtaking contrast to the lightly glazed kitchen cabinets. «

DESIGNER
Vicki Edwards CKD, ASID
Kitchen & Bath Images, LLC
1710 General George
Patton Dr., Suite 110
Brentwood, TN 37027
615.377.8771

SPECIAL FEATURES
Large island with raised center section housing microwave and warming drawer; custom hood with hand-carved molding, corbels; Venetian plaster; onyx mosaic backsplash

DIMENSIONS
20 x 19

PRODUCTS USED
Cabinetry: Cabinetry by Provines
Flooring: Stone
Countertops: Granite
Dishwashers: Bosch; Fisher & Paykel
Refrigerator: Sub-Zero
Wallcovering: Venetian plaster faux paint finish
Oven: Thermador
Cooktop: Thermador

MEMBER OF
SEN DESIGN GROUP

PHOTOGRAPHER: BILL LAFEVOR

Triumphal Arches

THIS AWE-INSPIRING NEW Italian-style home in north Nashville, Tennessee, boasts dramatic arches as a central motif throughout all spaces. Vicki Edwards, CKD, ASID, of Kitchen & Bath Images, LLC, used that theme to influence the kitchen's design elements.

The owners requested the inclusion of three tall arched windows, which consumed much of the wall space. Add to that their desire for a 60-inch Wolf range and an equally proportionate stone and copper hood, and it left very little wall space for cabinet storage.

The solution was an island, which supplies much of the storage, and a large pantry behind the range, which functions as a work space and an additional spot for stowing wares. These, along with tall cabinets on the available wall space, provide more than adequate storage. The island, with its radiused back and raised bar, is now one of the main focal points as well as the primary functioning work counter.

The bird's-eye maple and Brazilian cherry cabinets, zebrawood island top, granite, copper, and stone united beautifully as the space-defining elements and gave the room a unique quality and personality. Treesa Hudson, Allied ASID, the owners' interior designer, was instrumental in helping pull together the finishing details of the kitchen, which is now a triumph of grandeur and performance. «

DESIGNER
Vicki Edwards, CKD, ASID
Kitchen & Bath Images, LLC
1710 Gen. George Patton Drive, Suite 110
Brentwood, TN 37027
615.377.8771

SPECIAL FEATURES
Custom stone and copper hood, arched windows, radiused multilevel island, beveled leaded glass doors, custom Enkeboll Designs hand-carved posts and bar supports, zebrawood island preparation top

DIMENSIONS
20 x 23

PRODUCTS USED
Cabinetry: Cabinetry by Provines with bird's-eye maple perimeter and Brazilian cherry island
Flooring: Natural Jerusalem stone in random pattern
Countertops: Cashmere Gold granite on perimeter, Tropical New Vernice granite and Qwinique zebrawood on island
Sink(s): Native Trails hammered copper
Faucets: Dornbracht
Refrigerator: Sub-Zero
Range: Wolf 60-inch dual fuel
Hood: Stone Age Designs
Warming Drawer: Wolf
Microwave Drawer: Dacor
Dishwasher: ASKO, Fisher & Paykel
Ice Maker: Sub-Zero
Wallcovering: Faux paint finish
Leaded Glass Doors: Helios
Hardware: Top Knobs

MEMBER OF
SEN DESIGN GROUP

PHOTOGRAPHER: BILL LAFEVOR

Culinary Sophisticate

LOCATED IN WEST HARTFORD, Connecticut, the original culinary zone of this colonial-style home was a cramped galley kitchen that lacked storage. The homeowners enjoy visits from their children and friends, so they desired a space that was multifunctional, aesthetically pleasing, comfortable, and well-connected to its surroundings.

Lorey Cavanaugh, CKD/CBD, and the design team at Kitchen & Bath Design Consultants, LLC, devised a solution that included a multifunctional island. The piece incorporates a cooktop, seating, loads of storage, and a work station complete with file drawers. In order to connect the kitchen to the office and family room, an existing pass-through and wall separating the kitchen from the family room was removed, flooding the area with light from sliders leading to an outdoor seating area.

The new custom cabinets were painted in soft white and taupe enamel. Other aesthetic features include a custom handmade crackle-glazed tile on the kitchen backsplash and new hardwood flooring in rich, dark-stained red oak. Also notable are the mixed granite and engineered stone countertops, done in rich, earthy tones. The door style, crown molding, and carved corbels add to the design's overall luxurious aesthetic. Together, these elements create a serene and sophisticated atmosphere. «

DESIGNER
Lorey Cavanaugh, CKD/
CBD, and design team
Kitchen & Bath Design
Consultants, LLC
139 Vanderbilt Ave.
West Hartford, CT 06110
860.953.1101

SPECIAL FEATURES
Multilevel, multipurpose
island; soft, elegant
aesthetics in a muted,
rich color palette

DIMENSIONS
17 x 19

PRODUCTS USED
Cabinetry: Plain & Fancy
Medley with recessed
panel door in soft white
enamel for perimeter and
in taupe enamel for island
Flooring: Red oak with
black walnut stain
Countertops: Silestone
Amazon Leather for
perimeter, Brown Antique
granite for island
Sink(s): Elkay
Faucet: Kohler Vinnata
Refrigerator: GE
Monogram
Cooktop: GE Monogram
Hood: GE Monogram
Oven: GE Monogram
Dishwasher: GE
Monogram
Lighting: Pendant over
sink and baking center,
amber with etched
white opal glass
Wallcovering: Quemere
ceramic tile in Espresso
Crackle, Precious
Gems glass tile in Kona
Dolomite

MEMBER OF
SEN DESIGN GROUP

PHOTOGRAPHER: PLAIN & FANCY CUSTOM CABINETRY

Bright Ideas

THIS KITCHEN IN North Granby, Connecticut, was a full remodel with removal of the existing wall between the kitchen and mudroom/pantry. It involved relocation, enlargement and the addition of windows as well as enclosure of the back porch to make a new mudroom with additional storage. The wish list also called for a small breakfast bar with seating for three, more natural light, better ventilation and contemporary styling. The owners called on Charles Harrill of Kitchen & Bath Design Consultants LLC, who was perfectly poised for the project.

The original kitchen and mudroom/pantry areas were small and disjointed and storage was limited. A peninsula separated the kitchen and dining room but had cabinets above it, which cut out any available natural light and blocked the mountain view.

Harrill and his team reconfigured the layout, switching positions of all appliances. This allowed for a corner sink, with two new windows above it to capture the gorgeous views. A small window in the mudroom was closed up, creating a space for the refrigerator that is in close proximity to the cleanup and prep centers, and the window over the old sink was lengthened almost to the floor. Thrilled with the design, the homeowners have been cooking up a storm in their bright, new, visitor-friendly kitchen. «

DESIGNER
Charles Harrill
Kitchen & Bath Design
Consultants LLC
1000 Farmington Ave.
West Hartford, CT 06107
860.232.2872

SPECIAL FEATURES
Raised half-inch thick clear glass Starfire counter on breakfast bar; variegated glass mosaic accented with large format glass tiles; use of European cabinetry with a slab-shaped door in neutral tones; stainless steel finish on all hardware and fixtures

DIMENSIONS
20 X 12

PRODUCTS USED
Cabinetry: Ultracraft Thermofoil in Sakura Cherry, perimeter/ mudroom; Ultracraft Thermofoil in Blu Metallic, natural wood grain tall cabinets
Flooring: Satillo tile, kitchen/mudroom; porcelain tile, foyer
Countertops: SileStone in Ebony Pearl leather, perimeter; granite in Azul Platino, island
Sink(s): Kindred in stainless steel, primary, prep and bar
Faucets: Hansgrohe Solaris in Steel Optik, primary and prep
Dishwasher: KitchenAid
Range: KitchenAid
Lighting: Inner Fire Mini-Pendant by Tech Lighting
Refrigerator: KitchenAid
Backsplash: Lunada Bay glass tile, AKDO Reflections glass tile

MEMBER OF
SEN DESIGN GROUP

PHOTOGRAPHER: CHARLES HARRILL KBDC, DESIGN MANAGER/DESIGN ASSOCIATE; STEPHANIE LEHMAN KBDC, DESIGN ASSISTANT

Functional Elegance

THIS KITCHEN IN KAHALA, an exclusive neighborhood in Honolulu, was completely remodeled by Susan Palmer CKD, CBD of Susan Palmer Designs. The design needed to be modern yet complementary to the owner's antique Korean furniture that is displayed throughout the home. The space also needed to be accessible and organized, with multiple storage spaces and a great deal of counter space for cooking and prep. This family of four also entertains often, so the kitchen's layout had to be accommodating and highly livable.

During the process, there were a few challenges, such as overhead soffits and unusual existing construction and ducting systems. However, expert planning and innovative product solutions overcame each challenge.

The Pegaso Doors and sliding pantry exude uniqueness, as do the tempered glass counters and stainless steel counters. Magic corners and appliance garages were integrated to add functionality to the area, and the sleek Italian cabinetry intensifies the luxurious ambiance. As a special touch of safety, the countertops are hygienic surfaces such as glass and stainless steel, which inhibit bacterial growth typical of Hawaii's tropical climate. In the end, the family got just what they desired; an elegant space high on function and design. «

DESIGNER
Susan Palmer, CKD, CBD
Susan Palmer Designs
650 Iwilei Road, Suite 195
Honolulu, HI. 96817
808.599.7606

SPECIAL FEATURES
Sleek Italian cabinetry;
innovative materials;
high level of function

DIMENSIONS
11 x 13

PRODUCTS USED
Cabinetry: Pedini;
Integra Grey Oak
Flooring: Travertine
Countertops: Pedini glass
and stainless steel
Sink(s): Pedini Quadra
Faucets: KWC
Dishwasher: Miele
Cooktop: Bosch
Oven: Miele
Downdraft: Bosch

Soothing Style

RYAN GREY SMITH of Grey Design Studio worked hand-in-hand with these Seattle homeowners to help create their dream kitchen. Grey accomplished his clients' primary goal in the culinary space—to fashion a variety of modern details that fit well with the Northwestern aesthetic—by employing simple, clean-lined elements throughout the room. The finished result: a modern kitchen featuring a host of must-have conveniences.

Fascinating to the eye is the use of beautiful materials throughout the room. Smith employed solid, natural wood cabinets with integrated appliances. This integration lends the room its sleek appearance. The designer also retained the true form and color of all the materials in the room, which gives the kitchen an attractive contemporary style, as well as a soothing, natural quality. Granite countertops line the room and top the below-counter refrigerators, furthering the integrated styling. Stainless steel appliances and a concealed down-draft hood finish off the space. The final outcome is a well-designed kitchen that features various touches of the clients' personality throughout. «

DESIGNER
Ryan Grey Smith
Grey Design Studio
5136 N.E. 54th St.
Seattle, WA 98105
206.254.2223

SPECIAL FEATURES
Cabinet wood; art glass
screen in the windows;
integrated appliances

DIMENSIONS
14 x 22

PRODUCTS USED
Cabinetry: Rustic
American maple
Countertops: Granite
Flooring: End grain
fir flooring, Oregon
Lumber Co.
Sink: Kohler
Faucet: Grohe
Dishwasher: Asko
Cooktop: Wolf
Refrigerator: Wolf
Oven: Wolf Micro/Oven
built-in combo
Lighting: Lightolier
Backsplash: Granite

PHOTOGRAPHER: CHAD HOLDER

Bella Cucina

CRANSTON, RHODE ISLAND, home builder Bob Moll and partner Maria, of R&M Builders, wanted to create a workable kitchen that radiated the charm Maria fell in love with in Italy. Having worked with Right @ Home Design owner Richard Mooradian for years, Bob knew Mooradian was the ideal person to fashion an out-of-the-ordinary Tuscan-style cucina.

Mooradian's main challenge: fitting all the features into the 15x18 space. Inspired by Maria and Bob's input, though, Mooradian and his team accomplished the task in spades. They installed high-end Mouser Custom Cabinetry featuring Brookfield and Tiffany door styles in a burnished cherry accentuated by a merlot hue. The multilevel island entices guests to gather as the chef works at the L-shaped prep area. Installed at a higher-than-normal level, the Enkebol-adorned custom wood hood makes for a striking centerpiece. Mooradian topped off the spectacular space with an ornate hutch tucked away in a charming alcove.

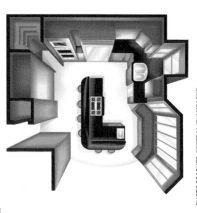

The secret to this project's overwhelming success? Meticulous planning, Mooradian says. "And the patient detail of construction installation that R&M Builders provided also helped bring the project to its performance of excellence," he notes. The intersection of both design angles resulted in the beautiful kitchen of Maria's every dream. «

DESIGNER
Richard Mooradian
Cheryl ConFreda
Right @ Home Designs
975 Charles St.
North Providence, RI
02904
401.726.8100

SPECIAL FEATURES
Tuscan styling inspired by the villas of Italy's Tuscan Valley, two-level island, hand-carved Enkebol-adorned hutch

DIMENSIONS
15 x 18

PRODUCTS USED
Cabinetry: Mouser Custom Cabinetry's Wood Bridge
Countertops: Imperial granite
Sink(s): Tumbled Crème Marfol by Walker Zanger
Faucets: Kohler
Refrigerator: Sub-Zero
Wallcovering: Venetian plaster
Other: Enkebol modlings and adornments

MEMBER OF
SEN DESIGN GROUP

PHOTOGRAPHER: SCOTT M. CHAMPAGNE

Cozy Condo

WITH MULTIPLE SPARE rooms in her dwelling, this homeowner had high expectations for her new Manhattan condo. Since she lives alone, entertains often and cooks regularly, she desired a spacious kitchen with a clean appearance and updated appliances. To meet her expectations, Derek Zylewicz of Urban Homes and designer Ellen Levy suggested a complete renovation. With his challenge before him—to create a fantasy kitchen in the previous location of the walk-in closet—Zylewicz was determined to create an exceptional cookery.

The previous space, which consisted of Formica cabinets arranged in an L-shape enclosed by walls, needed a complete overhaul. To blend the kitchen with its surroundings, Zylewicz removed and extended a majority of the wall into a U-shape. A peninsula multitasks as storage, seating and a space divider. For a chic appearance, the designer coupled Aster Cucine's wenge slab door cabinets with high-end stainless steel appliances. CaesarStone's Blizzard countertops engulf the base units, creating a sharp contrast of colors. Stainless steel toe kicks and hardware, complemented by glass upper cabinets, enhance the crisp appearance. A glass mosaic backsplash creates a brilliant array of tones. The space also includes matching stained oak floors, magic corners and the extension of the countertop to the floor. The room now serves as the client's dream kitchen. «

DESIGNER
Derek Zylewicz
Urban Homes
724 11th Ave.
New York, NY 10019
212.246.7700

SPECIAL FEATURES
Multitonal glass mosaic backsplash extends to the ceiling; magic corners; undercabinet lighting; countertop extends to the flooring; stained oak flooring to match cabinetry

DIMENSIONS
11 x 10.4

PRODUCTS USED
Cabinetry: Aster Cucine
Flooring: Stained oak to match cabinetry
Countertops: CaesarStone Blizzard
Sink(s): Franke
Faucet(s): Franke
Dishwasher: Bosch
Cooktop: Viking
Oven: Thermador
Hood: Sirius
Lighting: W.A.C
Refrigerator: Liebherr
Backsplash: Ann Sacks

MEMBER OF
SEN DESIGN GROUP

PHOTOGRAPHER: MICHAEL MCWERY

Modern Motives

THE BIGGEST CHALLENGE in this Brooklyn, New York, space was to create an ultramodern kitchen that blended with the ultratraditional appearance of the remainder of the house. To create the modern look, Derek Zylewicz and Laura Husni of Urban Homes Inc. selected slab door cabinets in teak wood, black lacquer and black-painted glass accented with stainless steel hardware. They also built one wall solely of tall units, including the refrigerator and freezer.

For an eye-appealing contrast, most appliances are stainless steel and all were built in. The countertop for the perimeter of the kitchen was done in a thin three-quarter-inch black absolute granite, while the island has a 2.5-inch-thick quartzite countertop. A horizontal theme was created throughout the kitchen to elongate the space. Even the teak grain runs horizontally. The quartzite countertop on the island has gray veins running horizontally and down the sides. A long, narrow, traditional-looking chandelier was placed above the island to further the horizontal effect.

Also enhancing the traditional aspects, the ceiling was raised in the center of the kitchen and lined with crown molding that matched the molding in several other rooms of the house. The rangetop and large hood also added to the traditional look.

DESIGNER
Derek Zylewicz and Laura Husni
Urban Homes Inc.
724 11th Ave.
New York, NY 10019
212.246.7700

SPECIAL FEATURES
Built-in appliances; custom-height cabinets; multilevel ceilings; exotic teak wood cabinets

DIMENSIONS
18 x 14

PRODUCTS USED
Cabinetry: Aster Cucine, Trendy Line, teak, black lacquer and black-painted glass
Countertops: Black Absolute granite; Luce Di Luna quartzite
Dishwasher: Asko; Fisher & Paykel
Cooktop: Wolf
Refrigerator: Sub-Zero
Oven: Wolf
Warming drawer: Wolf
Hood: Wolf

PHOTOGRAPHER: MICHAEL MOWERY

Big Apple Cookery

WITH HIS BUSY NEW YORK CITY LIFESTYLE, this homeowner has precious little time to cook a meal, let alone clean up afterward. He sorely needed an organized, functional space in which to relax and whip up a quick bite. To declutter his kitchen and make his home less hectic, the owner charged Melissa Intag of Urban Homes with the complete gut and renovation.

Her biggest roadblock: creating a sleek, modern look without disrupting the existing layout. Intag tackled the challenge by removing all the outdated materials and stand-alone appliances, which greatly improved the proportions and made way for a generous bank of new cabinets and accessories. The black-glass cube-shaped upper cabinets extend to the ceiling, while tall pull-out pantry units provide access in a snap. "Magic corners" and built-in appliances make quick work of dead spaces.

The juxtaposition of light oak with the stainless steel appliances and black counters and cabinets lends up-to-the-minute appeal and looks stunning against the existing marble floor. Undercabinet lights reflect off the stainless backsplash and counters, making up for the lack of direct light. With its host of user-friendly features and ramped-up pizzazz, this central-city kitchen lets the owner cook up fantastic food and unforgettable fun in a New York minute. «

DESIGNER
Melissa Intag
Urban Homes
724 11th Ave.
New York, NY 10019
212.246.7700

SPECIAL FEATURES
Absolute Black granite countertop to contrast the light European oak cabinets; undercabinet lighting; stainless steel backsplash

DIMENSIONS
18 x 11

PRODUCTS USED
Cabinetry: Aster Cucine
Flooring: Existing marble
Countertops: Absolute Black granite
Sink(s): Blanco
Faucets: Grohe Ladylux Plus
Dishwasher: Miele Incognito
Cooktop: Wolf 36-inch gas
Lighting: WAC undercabinet, Xenon fixtures, WAC pendant over island
Refrigerator: Sub-Zero
Wallcovering: Existing
Oven: Wolf
Hood: Miele
Microwave: Wolf
Wine reserve: GE Monogram

MEMBER OF
SEN DESIGN GROUP

Ample Antiquity

THESE HOMEOWNERS IN Distant Island, South Carolina, are exceptional cooks and frequent entertainers. They approached Barry Cutsler CKD of Kitchen Design Center with a specific goal: the quintessential Old World kitchen with all the advantages of the modern world. Their needs were definitive—considerable storage for cooking implements and food stuffs, along with ample room for wine and potables.

To accomplish this, Cutsler created a preparation area, wine refrigeration space and cache for small appliances and heavy cookware into a center island, offering a vintage furniture look similar to the living room. Designed in maple with a distressed and rubbed-through sesame finish, its Old World architectural details include corbels, inset panels and rustic hardware.

Next, two custom French country armoires were constructed in antiqued knotty pine with a centennial distressed finish to flank the cooking alcove. Bronze diamond mesh and glass insets placed in the door panels lend a distinctive quality and ambiance to the generous food and dinnerware storage. Surrounded by the arched bricks, the alcove incorporates a microwave drawer, range and additional cookware storage. «

DESIGNER
Barry Cutsler CKD
Kitchen Design Center
154 Robert Smalls
Parkway, Suite 2
Beaufort, SC 29906
843.521.1532

SPECIAL FEATURES
Cabinetry customized in design and materials to emulate old-world charm with modern conveniences; island offers a prep sink, wine storage and seating area

DIMENSIONS
13 x 19

PRODUCTS USED
Cabinetry: Corsi, pine wood; Luxor, maple
Flooring: Heart Pine
Countertops: Granite; Signature Custom Woodworking black walnut countertop, Waterlox tung oil finish
Sink(s): Bates and Bates, stainless steel; Link-A-Sink, copper
Dishwasher: Bosch
Cooktop: GE Profile, stainless steel
Hood: Dacor
Hood liner: Dacor
Oven: GE Profile with convection oven, stainless steel
Refrigerator: GE Mongram
Winecooler: GE Monogram

MEMBER OF
SEN DESIGN GROUP

Artistic in Asheville

ASHEVILLE, NORTH CAROLINA, is a locale known for its eclectic, energetic mix of art and architecture; it is an urban hot spot that emanates metropolitan vibrancy and small-town hospitality. Since these homeowners love to entertain, they desired a kitchen that might be as welcoming as their hospitable city of residence. To bring their dreams to fruition, they called on Larry Ficker and his design team at Cooper House Fine Cabinetry.

This home boasts stunning views of the surrounding landscape, and expansive decks adjacent to the kitchen provide the homeowners with an open-air entertaining venue. Inside the culinary space, a variety of details creates an inviting ambiance. Alectra Lyptus cabinets in auburn with a charcoal glaze by Dura Supreme line the perimeter of the room. Special features include a hutch/china cabinet and a black Alectra maple island featuring an espresso glaze and a red rub-through.

Ficker also designed the layout of the space for efficiency and to allow for ample traffic patterns. As a result, the homeowners can make quick work of small tasks even when guests come calling. The result is a well-designed kitchen that complements the stunning landscape, and the homeowners couldn't be more thrilled. «

DESIGNER
Larry Ficker
Cooper House
Fine Cabinetry
479 Hendersonville Road
Asheville, NC 28803
828.274.5414

SPECIAL FEATURES
Sunbury House doors on wall and base cabinets, and-on hutch/china cabinet; Alectra maple island with painted black espresso glaze

DIMENSIONS
16 x 18

PRODUCTS USED
Cabinetry: Dura Supreme Alectra
Countertops: Granite
Dishwasher: KitchenAid
Range: Five Star
Hood: Five Star
Oven: KitchenAid
Refrigerator: KitchenAid

MEMBER OF
SEN DESIGN GROUP

PHOTOGRAPHER: PAUL JEREMIAS

Heart of the Home

THE BUILDER AND HIS WIFE constructed this beautiful French Country home in Asheville, North Carolina, as a speculative build, and both desired the kitchen to be the gathering area. This meant integrating plenty of space so guests felt comfortable and, of course, making it extra eye-appealing. As such, the cabinetry and granite were to be a focal point in the room, exuding a definite wow factor.

Luckily there were minimal challenges during the entire process, allowing for extensive creative freedom. Working with Larry Ficker of Cooper House, the team decided to incorporate an oversized island, allowing plenty of area to prepare food, serve drinks and accommodate friends and family. They also worked to forge a detail-oriented design to punch up the kitchen's overall ambiance, and the island serves as a stunning focal point in the splendid space.

When the design was complete, there were many beautiful points of focus throughout the room, including the oversized island with turnposts and beadboard, the beaded inset cabinet style and the incredible range hood. Upon completion, the room was perfect from every angle and serves both form and function in this newly constructed home. «

DESIGNER
Larry Ficker
Cooper House
479 Hendersonville Road
Asheville, NC 28803
828.274.5414

SPECIAL FEATURES
Raised panel; maple beaded-inset with Sierra crackle-glaze cabinetry; maple hood and island, black, rubthrough and glaze, beadboard; turnposts and inset panels on island

DIMENSIONS
15 x 12

PRODUCTS USED
Cabinetry: Cooper House Custom by Rosewood Industries Inc.
Countertops: Granite
Sink(s): Elkay
Dishwasher: Bosch
Cooktop: Wolf
Refrigerator: Sub-Zero
Oven: Wolf
Warming drawer: Wolf
Microwave: Wolf

MEMBER OF
SEN DESIGN GROUP

PHOTOGRAPHER: PAUL JEREMIAS

Beaming with Beauty

THEIR ORIGINAL KITCHEN confined to cramped, closed-off quarters, this four-member Hudson, Massachusetts, family longed for an easy-to-navigate open-concept space that flowed seamlessly to the adjacent living and dining zones and also showcased the home's post-and-beam construction. No small undertaking, the from-scratch project necessitated a complete gut and remodel to actualize the client's every wish. Taking the helm of this complex redo was Mariette Barsoum, CKD, of Divine Kitchens.

Ensuring the now voluminous space transitioned effortlessly from one area to the next was Barsoum's foremost hurdle. To that end, the designer and her team incorporated the same flooring—antiqued hand-scraped maple—throughout the multi-themed milieu. To further boost the harmonious tone, Barsoum removed a half-wall that divided the kitchen and living room.

Barsoum also eliminated the restrictive half-wall at the basement stairway in the dining room and replaced it with a complementary banister—another aesthetically astute way she fashioned the now-airy arrangement. Other notable flourishes include the luxe granite countertops and the ultra-functional cabinetry, which comes in handy for storing both entertainment- and kid-related items! The grace note: The lofty ceiling, which reveals the lovely post-and-beam motif. Thanks to Barsoum's clever design solutions, this pretty-and-practical eat-play-live expanse is primed for parties big and small. «

DESIGNER
Mariette Barsoum, CKD
Divine Kitchens
40 Lyman St.
Westborough, MA 01581
508.366.5670

SPECIAL FEATURES
Post-and-beam-style home with an open ceiling exposing all the posts and beams, open-concept first floor

DIMENSIONS
11 x 11

PRODUCTS USED
Cabinetry: Holiday Kitchens Cabinetry
Flooring: Hand-scraped maple
Countertops: Peacock Green granite
Sink(s): Suneli
Faucets: Danze
Refrigerator: GE Profile
Range: GE Profile slide-in
Dishwasher: GE Profile
Wallcovering: Benjamin Moore paint

MEMBER OF
SEN DESIGN GROUP

PHOTOGRAPHER: LORETTA BERARDINELLI

At Its Best

THIS 14-YEAR-OLD KITCHEN underwent a complete remodel under the guidance of kitchen design expert Nicole M. Weiland of Casa Bella Design Center. In fact, the only elements that remained after the space was gutted were the large pantry and the tile flooring.

The most important objective of the new design was to improve upon storage space and increase appliance utility. The original appliance layout wasn't functional, and by removing unnecessary dividing walls, Weiland obtained the extra space needed to reconfigure the appliances. The oven, microwave, and range were relocated to more useful locations, and a larger-model refrigerator and prep sink were added.

The homeowners' original cabinetry was plentiful but needed a modern update. Weiland's solution? She incorporated a combination of roll-out trays, drawer storage, tray dividers, a cutting board, and space for spices into the cabinets.

Another important element was to improve upon the kitchen's style. Since the space is large, the designer was free to experiment with different finishes, colors, and textures. A mixture of medium-toned cherry and crème-painted cabinetry, paired with contrasting countertops, blends seamlessly with the roughly textured faux finish on the walls and the copper and orange accents in the backsplash tile. Molto bello! «

DESIGNER
Nicole M. Weiland
Casa Bella Design Center
15 W. Jefferson, Suite 103
Naperville, IL 60540
630.718.1440

SPECIAL FEATURES
Multilevel island, faux-finished walls with metallic and gold leaf, copper-accented backsplash, two-tone molding detail

DIMENSIONS
21 X 21

PRODUCTS USED
Cabinetry: Bertch Legacy Plus
Countertops: Zodiaq with Giallo Michelangelo on the perimeter and Rosso Verona on the island
Sink(s): Kohler
Faucet: Danze
Dishwasher: Fisher & Paykel
Range: Wolf
Lighting: Maxim
Refrigerator: Sub-Zero
Wallcovering: Custom faux finish, Daltile and American Olean tile backsplash
Oven: Thermador

MEMBER OF
SEN DESIGN GROUP

PHOTOGRAPHER: SHERMAN DUNNAM

DESIGNER
Haskell "Hank" Matheny, ASID
Sheila Stubbs
Haskell Interiors Design Collection
85 First St. N.E.
Cleveland, TN 37311
423.472.6409

SPECIAL FEATURES
Dual islands: one with beverage center and undercounter icemaker and another across from cooktop; refrigerator armoire with custom antiqued, leaded mirror fronts; mixed cabinetry; custom walnut hood

DIMENSIONS
27 X 14

PRODUCTS USED
Cabinetry: Jay Rambo in walnut and alder
Flooring: Oak
Countertops: Corian in kitchen, white marble in pantry
Sink(s): Oliveri
Faucets: Sigma
Refrigerator: Sub-Zero
Refrigerator Drawers: Sub-Zero
Icemaker: Sub-Zero
Cooktop: Wolf
Oven: Wolf
Microwave: Sharp drawers
Dishwasher: Bosch
Wallcovering: Schumacher
Backsplash: Calcutta Moonlight marble
Tile: Lyric Tile Co., Jerusalem limestone, Afyon Sugar marble

MEMBER OF
SEN DESIGN GROUP

Stylish Solutions

HASKELL "HANK" MATHENY, ASID, and Sheila Stubbs, both of Haskell Interiors Design Collection, transformed this space from a small den and kitchen area into a spacious culinary retreat. The home is located in a prestigious community and sits next to a small, tranquil pond on several acres.

The designers' biggest challenge was to incorporate the large number of kitchen gadgetry and other items into the space without the appliances taking center stage. To that end, all appliances featured integrated wooden doors and panels to disguise their placement. The ultimate example is the large armoire piece in the room, featuring a large freezer and separate refrigerator flanked by double pantries, dressed in walnut, with custom leaded antiqued mirror fronts and custom wood carvings.

Another challenge was separating the cooking space from the entertaining space. Two separate islands give the cook ample prep space, while a second beverage island with a secondary microwave, ice machine, and sink allows for guests to help themselves.

The homeowners also desired several cabinetry finishes, but they didn't want painted cabinets. The solution: to use walnut wood and stain as an accent for the armoire and hood, while bedecking the majority of the kitchen with alder wood sporting a medium brown finish. A perfect pairing! «

PHOTOGRAPHER: BRANDON HYDE, PERSPECTIVE PHOTOGRAPHY, CLEVELAND, TENNESSEE

Tidy in Tennessee

SITUATED HIGH ABOVE THE CITY OF CHATTANOOGA overlooking the Tennessee river, this kitchen belongs to a bachelor who tapped Hank Matheny of Haskell Interiors Design Collection with the challenge of creating a functional space for cooking and entertaining. Matheny's challenge: to create a user-friendly kitchen by transforming a small area in the corner of the existing living space. In addition, the client desired a traditional, uncluttered aesthetic with clean, simple lines.

To that end, Hank devised a layout, including two large full-height end cabinets that maximize the limited wall space and serve to hide the microwave and small appliances behind two hidden appliance garages. A large island serves as a spot for casual eating and a comfortable place to congregate during parties; it also contains several appliances.

The focal point of the space is a furniture piece that anchors the wall at the end of the living room and kitchen. Designed to look like an antique armoire, it contains both refrigerated and dry pantry space. While it fulfills the functional needs of the workspace, it also provides the owner with the uncluttered, "non-kitchen" look he desired. This bachelor now has a kitchen that integrates seamlessly into the elegant surroundings of his clean, classic home. «

DESIGNER
Haskell R. (Hank) Matheny, ASID
Haskell Interior Design Collection
85 1st St. N.E.
Cleveland, TN 37311
423.472.6409

SPECIAL FEATURES
Combo refrigerator/ pantry armoire; custom island brackets; microwave, appliance garages; limestone, glass plaque above cooktop

DIMENSIONS
12 x 16

PRODUCTS USED
Cabinetry: Showplace Cabinetry, Cherry Merlot, Ebony glaze; Cherry, charcoal stain (armoire)
Flooring: White oak
Countertops: Gallo Napoleon granite
Sink(s): Oliveri stainless steel
Faucets: Aquadis
Dishwasher: Bosch
Cooktop: Dacor
Lighting: Visual Comfort; task
Refrigerator: Sub-Zero
Wallcovering: Benjamin Moore paint
Oven: Dacor
Tile: Sonoma Tilemakers
Hardware: Top Knobs

MEMBER OF

SEN DESIGN GROUP

PHOTOGRAPHER: STEPHEN GREENFIELD

Open and Functional

Although these homeowners loved their home, they were ready to renovate the kitchen. The mandate: to turn the existing kitchen into a beautiful, open space in which to entertain friends and family with an Old World charm. The project scope included the kitchen and the adjoining butler's pantry and laundry room.

In the existing kitchen, the peninsula blocked one side of the room, creating a bottleneck during large gatherings. Additionally, the soffit over the sink wall was load-bearing and could not be removed. Catherine Goss of Nicely Done Kitchens went to work and provided the family with a kitchen that well exceeded their expectations.

A large, new island provides storage, a prep sink, a warming drawer and seating for two. It's also the gathering spot for friends and family. On the sink wall, cabinets tuck up under the soffit. Taller wall cabinets were used to frame the focal point of the kitchen, the range top and the hood. The addition of double pantries provided storage, framed the counter-depth refrigerator and housed the microwave. Recessed lighting in the raised ceiling and task lighting under the cabinets was integrated as well.

Fluting on the clipped sink and range bases accentuates the additional depth at the two open areas—the wide kitchen window and the stainless steel hood—creating a nice balance and rhythm within the space. «

DESIGNER
Catherine Goss
Nicely Done Kitchens
8934 Burke Lake Road
Springfield, VA 22151
703.764.3748

SPECIAL FEATURES
Limestone flooring and backsplash; refrigerator centered on pantries; clipped corners on sink base and range base; double ovens; island with prep sink and warming drawers

DIMENSIONS
17 X 14

PRODUCTS USED
Cabinetry: Holiday Kitchens
Flooring: Limestone
Countertops: Granite, Santa Cecelia
Sink(s): Elkay
Faucets: Grohe
Dishwasher: Miele
Rangetop: Wolf
Double ovens: Wolf
Lighting: Recessed in ceiling; undercabinet
Refrigerator: KitchenAid
Wallcovering: Painted faux finish
Wine cooler: Scotsman

MEMBER OF
SEN DESIGN GROUP

Island Paradise

THIS BEAUTIFUL GREAT FALLS, Virginia, home needed a bright new look in its dated kitchen, as well as a layout conducive to entertaining. Located on the main level, the kitchen, dining area and living room lacked the traffic flow the homeowners needed. To accomplish their remodeling goals, they turned to Sarah Clark of Nicely Done Kitchens.

After completely removing the main-level interior walls, Clark gave the space new life by exposing the shape of the cathedral ceiling. A large island with prep sink and bar-height seating wraps around the perimeter of the kitchen and living room. This creates a division of the space yet leaves the area open for interaction with guests. Another island, located in the center of the kitchen and directly across from the range, serves as the main prep area with a sink and additional seating. This island's organically shaped countertop lends a softness to the contemporary space.

The warm tones of the stained maple cabinets and wood floors, along with the sparkle of the granite countertops and glass tile backsplash, create exciting elements in the kitchen's clean design. The result is a stunning kitchen that is extremely functional and perfect for parties and impromptu get-togethers. «

DESIGNER
Sarah Anne Clark
Nicely Done Kitchens
8934 Burke Lake Road
Springfield, VA 22151
703.764.3748

SPECIAL FEATURES
Two islands, prep and cleanup; ceramic tile and Venetian glass backsplash; bookcase in island

DIMENSIONS
15 x 16

PRODUCTS USED
Cabinetry: Holiday Kitchens, Woodridge maple
Flooring: Maple wood
Countertops: Granite, Blue Pearl Royale
Faucets: Grohe
Range: AGA
Lighting: George Kovacs
Microwave: Sharp
Hood: Zephyr

MEMBER OF
SEN DESIGN GROUP

PHOTOGRAPHER: DARKO PHOTOGRAPHY

Dazzling Design

WHEN THE OWNERS OF THIS VIRGINIA HOME met with Catherine Goss of Nicely Done Kitchens about their culinary space, they had two specific problems to resolve: increase the amount of storage and plan for space for two people to work. Additionally, they wanted to coordinate the design with the contemporary look of the home.

Goss began by placing the sink on a diagonal, thus creating an additional work area facing the family room. She met the storage needs by locating two pantries on either side of the refrigerator. Goss also incorporated a bookcase in Coffee Bean finish to separate and unify the kitchen and family room. A floating glass countertop duplicates the ottoman in the family room and provides an eat-in area. Recessed lighting laid out in a uniform grid pattern highlights the work and eating zones.

Subtle attention to design details and functionality produced a kitchen that is a work of art. Stainless steel organic-shaped tiles behind the cooktop and a stainless steel hood create a focal point. Tuscan red paint seemingly pops the contemporary maple cabinets off the wall while softening the Grey Leather countertop. Sleek stainless steel handles complement the cabinets and mirror the appliance handles. Crown moulding and the light-rail moulding give the slab doors modern detail. The elements create a kitchen that exceeded the clients' expectations. «

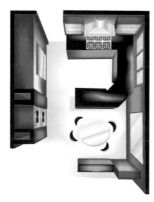

DESIGNER
Catherine Goss
Nicely Done Kitchens
8934 Burke Lake Road
Springfield, VA 22151
703.764.3748

SPECIAL FEATURES
Bookcase with storage located between the family room and kitchen; glass countertop at eat-in area; stainless steel backsplash

DIMENSIONS
13 x 16

PRODUCTS USED
Cabinetry: Holiday Kitchens
Countertops: Silestone
Faucet: Pegasus
Sink: Kohler
Appliances: GE Monogram
Hardware: Top Knobs

MEMBER OF
SEN DESIGN GROUP

High Stylings

THIS BRAND-NEW HOME in Oakland, California, had a traditional kitchen, which was unfitting of the homeowner's style. In fact, the client was so unhappy with the original design that they asked the builder to remove the original cabinetry before they moved in. Plus, this busy family of three wanted a kitchen that could be utilized by the whole family. The couple have a toddler-aged daughter, so they wanted some lower areas that she could reach easily.

Spencer Knight of Spencer Knight Kitchen Design dba Pedini of San Francisco was able to integrate a number of appliances and even cabinetry along the back wall, all while ensuring the space was aesthetically pleasing and flowed with style. The challenge involved ventilating the high-ceiling design, which Knight solved with aplomb by designing a soffit that extends out from the wall and then hanging the hood and lighting from it.

Glass lift-up doors at the sink provide separation, without looking too disconnected from the rest of the design. Stainless steel elements, such as the floating peninsula and soffit, give a clean-lined look. The completed project reflects each of the homeowner's desires and was the perfect fit for the family. «

DESIGNER
Spencer Knight
Spencer Knight Kitchen
Design dba Pedini of San
Francisco
675 Townsend St.
San Francisco, CA 94103
415.558.8178

SPECIAL FEATURES
Stainless steel peninsula;
multilevel counters;
stainless steel soffit;
glass lift-up doors

DIMENSIONS
15 x 15

PRODUCTS USED
Cabinetry: Pedini
Integra, Rift white oak,
Moro stain
Countertops: Stainless
steel, Calacata Oro, oak
Sink(s): Franke
Dishwasher: Miele
Steamer: Gaggenau
Cooktops: Gaggenau
Oven: Miele
Refrigerator: Sub-Zero
Microwave: Miele, lift-up

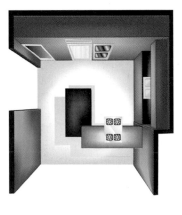

PHOTOGRAPHER: LISA SZE

Slim to Stunning

To remodel this kitchen in Laguna Niguel, California, Sandra T. Rodriguez CKD, Allied ASID of L&S Interiors borrowed eight feet from the patio to give the design the space it deserved. As the original area was twice as long as it was wide, it required precise planning to include each feature the homeowner desired, without causing it to appear crowded.

Rodriguez put cabinetry on both long ends to give the illusion that the room was shorter than it actually was. This set up the perfect canvas to incorporate a desk, an island, a table, a cleanup area and a cooking zone. By making the island wide, she also helped enhance the room's large yet cozy look.

The vaulted ceiling opened the space in volume, and the island now provides enough room for a group of eight to gather comfortably. The butcher block top makes preparation easy, as does the nearby sink built into the island. Behind the island, glass-fronted cabinetry makes everything simple to find. The separate prep and cleaning area enables the homeowners to work in the kitchen together. The final design also affords easy access to the barbecue area through French doors and provides a lovely view from the kitchen window. «

DESIGNER
Sandra T. Rodriguez CKD,
L&S Interiors
1130 N. Kraemer Blvd.,
Ste. D
Anaheim, CA 92806
714.998.8477

SPECIAL FEATURES
Multilevel island with built-in chopping block; built-in desk; glass and stone backsplash

DIMENSIONS
13 x 24

PRODUCTS USED
Cabinetry: Medallion Cabinets
Flooring: Casa Dolce Casa
Countertops: Kashmere Gold
Backsplash: Casa Dolce Casa Flagstone
Sink(s): Franke, Villeroy & Boch Fireclay Sinks
Dishwasher: Bosch
Cooktop: Thermador
Double oven: Thermador
Hood: Sirius

MEMBER OF
SEN DESIGN GROUP

PHOTOGRAPHER: STEVEN PAUL WHITSITT

Spaciously Updated

CONSTRUCTED THROUGHOUT SOUTHERN California by Joseph Eichler in the early 1960s, Eichler home styles are known for their open floor plans and ample amounts of natural light. These very attributes were exactly what CJ Lowenthal of Gilman Screens & Kitchens and Penn Chin of Elements in Design created within this kitchen space for her California homeowners. Boasting a flat roof style with no attic access, the home remodel was quite a challenge. Originally a galley kitchen, this renovated space now serves as a place for today's gracious style of living, as well as a spot to entertain a growing family.

To create a convenient, cozy, highly functional room, the designers incorporated a forced-air system within the cement foundation. They also added abundant storage and modern appliances, which bring the room to life and make usage highly convenient for the clients. Incorporated into the island is a wine refrigerator, warming drawer, microwave and recycling containers. Integrated appliances are concealed by means of roll-up and full overlay doors. Hidden roll-out spice cabinets flank each side of the cooktop. A Haffale pantry system allows for maximum storage. The final product is in an updated, spacious room designed to accommodate a busy family. «

DESIGNER
CJ Lowenthal
Gilman Screens &
Kitchens
1031 E. Hillsdale Blvd.
Foster, City, CA 94404
650.286.0433

Penny Chin
CID, ASID, NKBA
Elements in Design
650.400.4900

SPECIAL FEATURES
Integrated wine
refrigerator, warming
drawer, recycling
containers; hidden
roll-out spice cabinets;
Haffale pantry system

DIMENSIONS
16 x 21

PRODUCTS USED
Cabinetry: Dura
Supreme
Faucet: KWC
Refrigerator: Sub-Zero
Cooktop: Wolf
Oven: Thermador
Hood: Wolf
Dishwasher: Miele
Compactor: KitchenAid
Disposal: Franke
Microwave: GE
Undercounter
refrigerator: Viking
Countertops: Granite,
available at Gilman
Screens & Kitchens
Flooring: Ceramic
porcelain tile
Sink: Fireclay
Backsplash: Torreon
tumbled stone

MEMBER OF
SEN DESIGN GROUP

PHOTOGRAPHER: MERT CARPENTER

Flattering Imitation

AVID ENTERTAINERS AND the parents of two young daughters, these Burlingame, California, homeowners desired a culinary space that might beautifully function as the heart of their home. To transform their existing ranch-style kitchen into a grand creation, they called on the expertise of Kathy Smith at Gilman Screens & Kitchens, the same designer who had previously renovated the husband's mother's kitchen.

The client desired a spacious, grand ambiance that might comfortably fit a table and chairs, as well as a furniture hutch with glass cabinet. She also requested that the kitchen be similar in appearance to her mother-in-law's while retaining a level of individuality. To best achieve this, Smith selected the same color palette throughout. She then incorporated signature style by installing a different type of door. She also opted for a unique treatment on the grand, multilevel island, accents and molding detail.

Smith installed an integrated, ornate hood to anchor the space; the hood also serves as a stunning focal point. When completed, the newly renovated kitchen exuded its own distinctive ambiance while also boasting a striking resemblance to the client's mother-in-law's cookery. In this case, it seems imitation truly is the sincerest form of flattery. «

DESIGNER
Kathy E. Smith
Gilman Screens
& Kitchens
217 California Drive
Burlingame, CA 94010
650.340.2890

SPECIAL FEATURES
Integrated hood;
multilevel island

DIMENSIONS
16 x 20

PRODUCTS USED
Cabinetry: Dura
Supreme, Nob Hill door,
Antique White with
Espresso glaze on maple
Flooring: Santos
mahogany prefinished
Countertops: Antique
Brown granite; Calcutta
Vagli, island
Sink(s): Julien
Faucets: Rohl Perrin
Dishwasher: Bosch with
panel
Range: Dacor
Refrigerator: Sub-Zero
with panels and RKI
handles
Hardware: Schaub

MEMBER OF
SEN DESIGN GROUP

Storage Galore

THIS KITCHEN IN Foster City, California, was a complete remodel, as the original kitchen was expanded into a courtyard and then attached to the garage.

CJ Lowenthal of Gilman Screens & Kitchens was ready for challenge. First, the team constructed a 26-foot wall and made sure the space accommodated the decorative cabinet door style chosen by the homeowners. To ensure the wall of cabinets balanced the busyness of the doors, the lower cabinets were designed with a contemporary twist—full-height doors with rollout shelves and drawer banks.

The mixed media floor adds another interesting facet to the design. Using travertine and Brazilian cherry, the flooring combines contemporary stylings with the warmness of wood—just as the cabinets do—to bring the entire room together.

The homeowners like to entertain and now have an open-flow lower level that is conducive for large parties. The two-level island is ideal for meals and for serving guests during a get-together.

The wall was visually broken up with a large hood, an open bookcase cabinet, microwave and oven. Two small pantries next to the refrigerator include pullouts for food storage. A stone and glass backsplash adds another element of personal style to the space. Another set of cabinets, tucked handily below the stairs, provides extra storage space. «

DESIGNER
CJ Lowenthal
Gilman Screens & Kitchens
1031 E. Hillsdale Blvd.,
Ste. D
Foster City, CA 94404
650.286.0433

SPECIAL FEATURES
Stone and glass backsplash with copper colors; two-level island; eat-in kitchen; wood and stone floor; cherry cabinets

DIMENSIONS
22 x 12

PRODUCTS USED
Cabinetry: Dura Supreme, Venice door in cherry ginger
Flooring: Travertine, Brazilian cherry
Countertops: Granite, Monticello
Dishwasher: KitchenAid
Cooktop: Viking Rangetop
Refrigerator: Thermador
Oven: Thermador
Microwave: GE Spacemaker
Trash compactor: KitchenAid

MEMBER OF
SEN DESIGN GROUP

PHOTOGRAPHER: CYNTHIA LARSON

Expanded Elegance

THIS KITCHEN SPACE in Dorset, Vermont, needed to be expanded to accommodate the homeowners' lifestyle. The current construction was too tight and didn't function well enough to let the cooks enjoy preparing a meal. The new design also had to be large enough to suit the three generations living in the home. This meant plenty of seating and a smooth transition from zone to zone.

Before the designer, Craig Angstadt of R.K. Miles, Inc., got to work, he had to a plan a project that would not only meet all the family's requests but also attain the proper style and finish to blend with the home. Collaborating with the homeowners and the contractor, Angstadt was able to devise the perfect design.

To ensure the appliance utility was maximized, the designer installed two sinks, two cooktops, and two dishwashers into the space. A 48-inch Sub-Zero refrigerator and 32-inch flat screen TV were also added. The result was two separate and complete cooking areas, with an entertainment zone for the cooks to share. The TV also is viewable from the large island, which is designed as an area for the family to gather and enjoy each other's company.

Eye-catching details, such as the honed granite countertops and lighting in the glass door cabinets, made the project a complete success. «

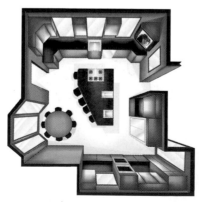

DESIGNER
Craig Angstadt
R.K. Miles, Inc.
P.O. Box 1125
Manchester Center, VT
05255
802.362.1952

SPECIAL FEATURES
Very large island; dual sinks, dishwashers, cooktops; honed granite countertops; lighting in glass door cabinets with glass shelves and beadboard backs; flat-screen TV; custom-painted and glazed finish; wood beams

DIMENSIONS
20 x 21

PRODUCTS USED
Cabinetry: Vermont Custom Cabinetry
Flooring: Pumpkin Pine in Carlisle wide plank
Countertops: Honed Absolute Black granite
Sink(s): Kindred for main, Blanco for bar
Refrigerator: Sub-Zero
Cooktops: Wolf
Double Oven: Thermador
Warming Drawer: Thermador
Dishwashers: Bosch
Wallcovering: Paint

MEMBER OF
SEN DESIGN GROUP

PHOTOGRAPHER: STEPHEN GOODHUE

Space with Grace

HAVING JUST MOVED from Texas, these clients usually loved wide open spaces, but not in the kitchen of their newly acquired home. While the existing kitchen was large, it was not functional, lacking storage, counter space and an eating bar. It also needed a baking center, deep counter work space, and a small desk area.

The new design by Joy Dolling AKBD, NKBA of Eileen Schoener Design, Inc., included two full-height pantries with full-extension pull-out drawers. A large spice pull-out is conveniently placed next to the cook top.

The existing island was designed to house a cooktop, without compromising workspace or livability. The large granite slab boasts a detailed edge. Removing the existing desk allowed room for the baking center, including the ovens, storage, display, and work areas. The designers achieved the new, smaller desk area by wrapping the new counter around an existing corner on the opposite side of the kitchen.

To complement the warm wood tones, Interior Designer Eileen Schoener, Allied ASID, selected a unique slab with crystal insets, a hand painted tile for the backsplash, a Murano, blown glass pendant, and a coral with sage tapestry for the rustic iron barstools. Everything came together to give the clients the kitchen of their dreams. «

DESIGNER
Joy Dolling AKBD, NKBA
Eileen Schoener Design, Inc.
1449 130th Ave. N.E.
Bellevue, WA 98005
425.450.9055

SPECIAL FEATURES
Arched valances,
oversized island

DIMENSIONS
16 x 16

PRODUCTS USED
Cabinetry: ESD, Inc. Custom
Flooring: Wood
Countertops: Slab
Sink(s): Franke
Faucet: Grohe
Dishwasher: GE Profile,
stainless steel
Cooktop: GE Profile,
stainless steel
Lighting: Crystal
Refrigerator: GE Profile,
stainless steel
Oven: GE Profile,
stainless steel

Strong Storage

To GIVE THESE Florida homeowners the kitchen of their dreams, they needed plenty of storage and functional zones. The homeowners have grown children, but during the holidays, the whole family—and even their friends— loves getting together to enjoy each other's company. So they needed new functionality in a formerly outdated space. To make sure the job was done right, they called on Chris Guccione of Gucci Interiors Inc. to fully remodel their cook's nook.

To make culinary duties simpler, all drawers are full extension, and pull-out spice shelving is located in select wall cabinets. Some very special engineering went into this design process to ensure all the additions not only looked great but would prove sturdy and safe for years to come, as well. To provide these homeowners with pantry cabinets and a wine cooler, the designers had to remove a load-bearing column/wall that supported the ceiling trusses.

After removal, the load had to be transferred to the other walls on both sides of the new built-in area. An engineer was brought in for this process, and in the end, the redesign was a complete success! The designers were able to devise a resourceful solution for the desired design, and the homeowners are having more fun than ever celebrating the holidays at home. «

DESIGNER
Chris Guccione
Gucci Interiors Inc.
1907 W. Copans Road
Pompano Beach, FL
33064

SPECIAL FEATURES
Full-extension shelving,
pull-out spice shelving

DIMENSIONS
14 x 10

PRODUCTS USED
Cabinetry: Diamond
Flooring: Ceramic
Countertops: Granite
Sinks: Kohler
Faucets: Delta
Refrigerator: LG
Oven: GE Profile
Dishwasher: GE Profile
Microwave: GE Profile

MEMBER OF
SEN DESIGN GROUP

PHOTOGRAPHER: LARA STERN

A Catered Affair

A SMALL FAMILY, these Longport, New Jersey, homeowners are big-time entertainers. While their former kitchen was a pleasant spot, it didn't provide the square footage needed to throw fabulous fetes. So they hired Albert J. DeNovellis of B&B Kitchens to gut the room and transform it into a modern caterers' kitchen that also would function well even when the client wasn't hosting a glammed-up get-together.

In order to stock the space with every cuisine-related element under the sun, DeNovellis incorporated an extra-large range top, a built-in steamer, a commercial ventilation, a service island, and an oversized main island. Cutlery drawers, utensil drawers, and roll-out trays make accessing tableware a snap. To provide a place to do paperwork and consult the evening's menu, DeNovellis integrated a nifty nook-style lap drawer/sitting area into the main island. A second island doubles as a wet bar for guests in the adjacent room and includes a sink and dishwasher, as well as easy access to the wine fridge.

Located handily between the refrigerators, the beverage/snack center features a Miele coffee system, hidden recycling receptacle, glass and dish storage, recessed wall drawers, small utensil drawer, microwave drawer, and a buffet cabinet—all within reach of the prep area under the coffee unit.

Custom trim and soffits, stainless steel accents, maple, and exotic anigre veneers round out the catered-for-them composition—a setup that satisfies the clients' every whim and makes celebrating a breeze. «

DESIGNER
Albert J. DeNovellis
B&B Kitchens
4273 N. Delsea Drive
Newfield, NJ 08344
856.794.9009

SPECIAL FEATURES
Exotic veneered cabinetry, custom steel and wood work, abundant conveniences throughout, in-counter steaming and ventilation

DIMENSIONS
20 X 24

PRODUCTS USED
Cabinetry: Holiday Kitchens' IDC frameless with Frisco door style and quartered figured anigre with maple edge-banding
Faucets: Grohe
Sinks: Elkay
Countertops: Chocolate granite
Refrigerators: Sub-Zero, Sub-Zero Tall Wine
Range: Viking
Ovens: Wolf double built-in
Ventilation: Viking pro hood, Gaggenau telescopic swivel downdraft system
Dishwashers: Asko, Miele
Microwave: Sharp microwave drawer
Other: Miele built-in coffee system, Gaggenau Vario electric in-counter steamer, KitchenAid compactor, custom stainless steel by Kiker Sheet Metal Corp.

MEMBER OF
SEN DESIGN GROUP

PHOTOGRAPHER: ROBERT DECRESCENZO, ROBERT ALAN STUDIO

Tuscany at Topsail

SITUATED ON VIRGINIA CREEK just off Topsail Island, N.C., is this exquisite estate house with a kitchen of Tuscan influence. To make their dream a reality, the homeowners contacted William N. Nesbitt of Shoreline Cabinet Company. Nesbitt successfully brought the homeowners' desires to fruition by fashioning a warm, inviting culinary space that is both casual and homey. A large brick arch around the cooktop serves as the primary focal point and gives the feel of an old brick oven; the arch is complemented by the pass-through on the opposite wall. A simple door design composed of cherry with warm paprika stain and several heavy turned posts further enhances the Old World style.

To top off the beautiful details inside, both the clients and designer opted to take full advantage of the glorious views of Virginia Creek outside. They achieved this by placing the sink in a large island facing the water. Now it doesn't matter the weather, the home-owners will be able to take advantage of a panoramic view of the property while they prepare a meal for friends and family. Also included in the island are display areas for items the clients have collected over the years. Nesbitt created the areas by placing a bookcase between the fireplace and brick arch. The result is an exceptional space that exceeded the client's expectations. «

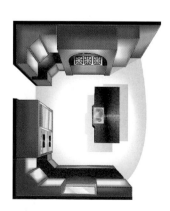

DESIGNER
William N. Nesbitt
Shoreline Cabinet
Company
2725 I-D Old Wrightsboro
Road
Wilmington, NC 28405
910.772.1411

SPECIAL FEATURES
Brick arch around
cooktop; display areas;
fireplace

DIMENSIONS
15 x 18

PRODUCTS USED
Cabinetry: Dura
Supreme
Flooring: Brazilian cherry
Countertops: Verde Jade
granite
Sink(s): Elkay
Dishwasher: Bosch
Cooktop: Dacor
Refrigerator: KitchenAid
Oven: KitchenAid
Microwave: KitchenAid

MEMBER OF
SEN DESIGN GROUP

PHOTOGRAPHER: DAN BAILEY

Views of Villagio

WHEN MARK AND KELLY BATSON of Tongue & Groove came to designer Neal Nesbitt of Shoreline Cabinet Company, they had some very distinct ideas about the kitchen for their home they called "Villagio De Batsone."

They wanted to mix old with new, so the team got to work, deciding first on a slab cherry door with a deep cocoa brown stain for the perimeter. Contemporary stainless feet and an inset knotty distressed ginger alder were chosen for the island.

The perimeter tops are Botticino marble with an eased edge. A two foot high backsplash accents an interesting feature: no wall cabinets throughout the entire kitchen. Instead, the homeowners' collection of artwork adorns the walls, and additional storage is provided in the adjoining 8-feet of pantry space, which features opaque glass doors.

The island features a sculptured ogee edge and drain board grooves. The island's cabinetry brings in an Old World feel, displaying heavy distressing, bunn feet, a fireclay farm sink and inset doors with wrought iron handles. The island transitions into a table with large round legs and a 3-inch thick table top—the perfect place for the family to gather.

Now, standing at the sink in the island, the view of the back patio through solid glass walls is as beautiful as the homeowners' new stunning kitchen. «

DESIGNER
William Neal Nesbitt
Shoreline Cabinet
Company
2725 Old Wrightsboro
Road, Suite 1-D
Wilmington, NC 28405
910.772.1411

SPECIAL FEATURES
24-inch marble
backsplash; 6 x 9 island;
no wall cabinets; kitchen
perimeter contemporary
with inset heavy
distressed alder island;
top combination of alder
wood and Botticino
marble

DIMENSIONS
16 x 18

PRODUCTS USED
Cabinetry: Dura
Supreme, Camden
Cherry Coco Brown
perimeter with Arcadia
inset heavy Heirloom
Sage; Coffee glaze knotty
alder, island
Countertops: Botticino
marble by Carolina
Creations; distressed
alder by Signature
Custom Woodwooking,
island tabletop
Sink(s): Shaw, farm sink;
Elkay, prep sink
Range: Wolf
Refrigerator: Sub-Zero
Wine cooler: Sub-Zero

MEMBER OF
SEN DESIGN GROUP

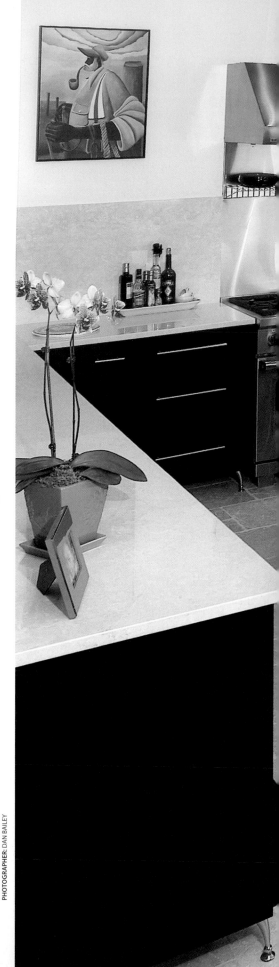

PHOTOGRAPHER: DAN BAILEY

Open and Bright

THIS SAN JOSE, CALIFORNIA, homeowner wanted a warm and inviting kitchen with an open floor plan and functional workspace. Another request was to transform the dark, dated kitchen into a light, open space while keeping the window in the existing location and creating additional storage. The client called on Lisa Cross of Gridley Company to complete the kitchen remodel.

The outdated soffit was removed to give higher ceilings to the space, which added 12 inches in height, instantly making the room feel larger and more open. It also provided additional cabinet storage. Additionally, the designer removed a run of wall cabinets and added an island to create a better flow in the room. The use of natural materials and the neutral colors makes the space feel warm and inviting. A blend of general, task and accent lighting was added to provide the most pleasant and functional illumination possible.

The oak cabinets were replaced with painted, frameless construction cabinets. This not only brightened the look of the kitchen but also addressed the client's request for additional storage. Adding an island achieved an open traffic flow and created additional work space. Also, a display cabinet, located on the other side of the island, showcases the client's cookbooks and special pieces. «

DESIGNER
Lisa Cross
Gridley Company
122 Orchard City Drive
Campbell, CA 95008
408.374.0900

SPECIAL FEATURES
Lyptus wood cabinets on island; four-part heirloom distressed-painted cabinets; custom-designed valance over sink and hutch for displaying plates

DIMENSIONS
12' x 14'

PRODUCTS USED
Cabinetry: Dura Supreme, Alectra Series, antique white with espresso glaze
Hardware: Hafele
Flooring: Solid oak
Countertop: Natural stone
Sink(s): Kohler
Faucet: Delta, Brizo
Dishwasher: KitchenAid
Compactor: KitchenAid
Cooktop: Thermador
Lighting: Tech Lighting Elements
Refrigerator: KitchenAid
Filtration system: Everpure
Oven: KitchenAid
Wallcovering: Kelly-Moore paint

White at Home

THIS KITCHEN REMODEL in Chattanooga, Tennessee, was serious business, as the design team gutted it down to the studs to accommodate a new layout and appliance placement. And the design hit especially close to home for designer Becky Worley—literally!—as the remodel was her own kitchen.

After a few years of serious cabinetry consideration, she chose the classic stylings of a white-painted kitchen with an inset door. The honed Calcutta Gold Marble countertops are as beautiful as the full-custom cabinetry they reside upon. Walker Zanger's Heirloom White Tile contributes to the timeless design. By putting a darker stain on the hardwood floors and using Plato's Fog Blue painted finish for the island's raised panel beaded inset style, Worley kept the room looking cozy.

The former kitchen was dark with a wide island and poorly planned space, making it feel small and cramped. To open it up to accommodate two cooks, the new center island is longer than before and more narrow for wider passage. A second prep sink adds to the functionality. Worley gave the double-hung window over the sink a makeover by replacing it with a leaded glass window. She also took the white cabinetry to the ceiling, with lighted glass doors at the top level that make this design shine brighter than ever before. «

DESIGNER
Becky Worley
Classic Cabinetry
2525 Broad St., Ste. 101
Chattanooga, TN 37408
423.266.0077

SPECIAL FEATURES
Double-door wall cabinets to ceiling; custom wood hood; two paint finishes; honed marble tops with laminated edge on island; leaded glass window

DIMENSIONS
16 x 24

PRODUCTS USED
Cabinetry: Plato Woodwork, Diamond White and Fog painted finishes
Flooring: Red oak hardwood
Countertops: Honed Calcutta gold marble
Sink(s): Shaw's original fluted front apron; Kohler
Faucets: Rohl
Dishwasher: Viking
Cooktop: Viking
Oven: Viking
Microwave: Viking
Warming drawer: Viking
Lighting: Recessed, Xenon undercounter
Refrigerator: Viking
Hot water dispenser: InSinkErator
Ice maker: Scotsman
Backsplash tile: Walker Zanger; Gramercy Park

MEMBER OF
SEN DESIGN GROUP

PHOTOGRAPHER: BRAD CANSLER

Set in Stone

THE HOMEOWNER IN CHATTANOOGA, TENNESSEE, presented the designer with the challenge of incorporating a full stone wall in the kitchen, as well as the desire to showcase multiple warm-toned finishes.

Becky Worley of Classic Cabinetry accomplished the task by fully incorporating the range, hood, base and wall cabinetry of the range area under an arch and then pulling the stone wall forward to incorporate 24-inch-deep storage cabinetry, drawers, a microwave and warming drawer.

A mixture of distressed paint, glaze and rustic alder with stain and glaze finishes adds to the warmth of the room. The multiple colors in the ceramic glass mosaic tiles on the backsplash and in the stone wall create even more dimension throughout the space.

A second challenge was keeping the kitchen open and cozy for the whole family, but also comfortable and accessible enough for a single cook. This was accomplished by creating an inviting space for visitors on the seating side of the island, while keeping the sink, range and appliances within easy range for the cook. Ample storage space in the butler's pantry keeps additional dinnerware and serving pieces close at hand, but tucked neatly out of the way as well. «

DESIGNER
Becky Worley NKBA
Classic Cabinetry
2525 Broad St., Ste. 101
Chattanooga, TN 37408
423.266.0077

SPECIAL FEATURES
Cabinetry incorporated into stone wall; multiple cabinetry and countertop finished; multilevel island

DIMENSIONS
15' x 22'

PRODUCTS USED
Cabinetry: Plato Woodwork, Atlanta Full Overlay Door style, Diamond White, Rustic Alder
Butler's pantry: Plato Woodwork, Coventry Beaded inset door style, Charcoal
Flooring: Red oak hardwood
Countertop: Granite, Copa Cabana, island; concrete, range
Sink(s): Kohler
Faucets: Kohler
Hot water dispenser: InSinkErator
Dishwasher: Bosch
Range: Viking
Lighting: Xenon undercabinet
Refrigerator: Sub-Zero
Wallcovering: Benjamin Moore paint, Umber Glaze
Microwave: Viking
Warming drawer: Viking
Trash compactor: KitchenAid

MEMBER OF
SEN DESIGN GROUP

Designer's Dream

AFTER PUTTING HER expertise to work in countless kitchens for others, Susan Klimala, CKD, of The Kitchen Studio of Glen Ellyn, was ready to take on her newest client: herself.

As part of the whole-house gut remodel of the 1950s Colonial home that she shares with her family of five in Glen Ellyn, Illinois, Klimala wanted to create a large functional kitchen with plenty of room for multiple cooks to move around. At the same time, she wanted to ensure the space could also serve as a focal point for entertaining.

Having a lot of light in the space was important, so Klimala started the design by placing three large windows over the kitchen sink. Next, she created a comfortable and casual eating area where she could enjoy daily meals together with her husband and kids. She also added a variety of unique touches to truly make the space their own, including a built-in banquette with antique stained-glass panels, a custom arched wood-and-plaster hood, and a cherry butcher-block top for the island.

In the end, the only thing that matters is if the client is pleased, and Klimala and her family couldn't be happier with their new culinary dream come to life. But they aren't the only ones impressed with the design. In fact, this kitchen won a National NKBA award for large kitchens in 2005, and it is the backdrop of the NKBA's current national ad campaign. «

DESIGNER
Susan Klimala, CKD
The Kitchen Studio of Glen Ellyn
522 Crescent Blvd.
Glen Ellyn, IL 60137
630.858.4848

SPECIAL FEATURES
Built-in banquette with antique stained glass windows, trio of windows centered over the sink, custom wooden hood, rustic brick tile backsplash

DIMENSIONS
17 x 15

PRODUCTS USED
Cabinetry: Woodharbor Somerlake door in Coastal White
Flooring: Oak
Countertops: Soapstone
Sink(s): Kohler Hawthorne double bowl
Faucets: Newport Brass in satin nickel
Refrigerator: Viking 42-inch
Range: Viking 36-inch dual fuel
Ventilation: Zephyr Tornado II insert
Dishwasher: Viking
Wallcovering: Sherwin-Williams paint
Other: Plugmold outlet strips

MEMBER OF
SEN DESIGN GROUP

Chef's Convenience

WHEN THIS CALIFORNIA couple contacted Deborah Nassetta of Roomscapes Inc., they had a gutted kitchen remodel in the plans for their culinary space. Although the clients are the homeowners, the couple's personal chef also had specific requests regarding the kitchen's new design. To meet the chef's primary requirement, designer Deborah Nassetta created a large plating area, adding personality to the space and convenience for the chef.

Since the location of the range creates minimal storage space, Nassetta added window shelves to compensate for the shortcomings. Providing ease of use, Nassetta installed double sinks and dishwasher drawers. This allows all users of the cooking area to speed through the cleanup. Providing a mainstay and visual interest to the room is the 10-foot island, beautifully topped with a Spekva walnut wood top. Conveniently located, pantries are installed on either side of the Sub-Zero refrigerator. This again adds more storage space, a highly coveted feature of most kitchens. At the project's conclusion, the layout works exceptionally for the client, designer and chef. «

DESIGNER
Deborah Nassetta,
CKD CBD
Roomscapes Inc.
23811 Aliso Creek Road
Suite 139
Laguna Niguel, CA 92677
949.448.9627

SPECIAL FEATURES
Dual sinks, dishwashers;
10-foot island with prep
sink

DIMENSIONS
14 x 22

PRODUCTS USED
Cabinetry: Wood-Mode
Inc.
Countertops: Carrara
marble, Spekva walnut
island top
Sinks: Kohler
Faucets: Kohler
Dishwasher: Fisher &
Paykel
Cooktop/range: Wolf
Refrigerator: Sub-Zero
Wallcovering: Paint
Microwave: KitchenAid
Hood: Wolf

MEMBER OF
SEN DESIGN GROUP

PHOTOGRAPHER: LARRY FALKE

Timeless Design

THIS NEWPORT BEACH, CALIFORNIA, homeowner had recently purchased and gutted this entire home in order to change the configurations and space planning throughout. The homeowner's original intention was to create a wonderful place to live for a few years and then to turn it over for resale.

The biggest challenge was the homeowner's desire to create a space with appealing views from both the newly opened living room area, as well as to fashion a floor plan that would attract buyers on the resale market. This transitional kitchen was created to achieve this desire, with clean lines and simple details to present a tailored look.

Wrapped columns and beams were designed to separate the kitchen from casual dining and living spaces overlooking the golf course below. Both the owner and designer worked to create a feeling of ease and symmetry in the space. The large cooking area is flanked with ribbed glass "dish pantry" cabinets, creating a cooking alcove with both a 48-inch range and prep sink. Overscaled white shaker door cabinetry was selected for the space. The beautiful design, fitted with large walkways and pantries that extend to the counters, accommodates the residents' every need. «

DESIGNER
Tawnya Coleman CKD, CBD
Roomscapes Inc.
23811 Aliso Creek Road, #139
Laguna Niguel, CA 92677
949.448.9627

SPECIAL FEATURES
Cooking alcove; glass and open display in the nook cabinetry; detailed wrapped column/beam

DIMENSIONS
24' x 14'

PRODUCTS USED
Cabinetry: Wood Mode, Sonoma recessed door style
Dishwasher: Viking; Kitchen Aid drawers
Refrigerator: Viking
Wallcovering: Paint
Range: Viking
Hood: Viking
Microwave: Wolf

MEMBER OF
SEN DESIGN GROUP

PHOTOGRAPHER: STEVEN PAUL WHITSITT

Entertaining with Ease

A COUPLE WHO LOVE to entertain, the homeowners of this Laguna Niguel, California, dwelling desired a kitchen with appliances fit for an avid cook. To design a gourmand's dream space, the homeowners called on the design team at Roomscapes Inc. Eager to create a well-crafted space to suit their clients' needs, the designers began by gutting the room and removing the soffits.

To accommodate an array of appliances, the design team incorporated a wine storage area into the family room, thus leaving additional space in the kitchen. They also selected a 48-inch range and a microwave drawer by Sharp, which satisfactorily saves functional countertop space.

Atop the island, the designers installed a dramatic slab of granite. Contemporary-styled pendants hang above from a curved rail system. An appliance garage situated between the refrigerator and coffee maker makes effective use of the angled space. A glass mosaic tile backsplash by Oceanside glass was a custom gradient blend; the backsplash adds visual interest to the room. A floating lighted shelf suspended above a window provides additional task and accent lighting. Once their new kitchen was completed, the homeowners found an efficient, inviting space designed to host an array of friends and family. «

DESIGNER
Ginger Brewsaugh
Roomscapes Inc.
23811 Aliso Creek Road,
Ste. 139
Laguna Niguel, CA 92677
949.448.9627

SPECIAL FEATURES
Range alcove with gradient blend mosaic tile backsplash; olive ash burl inset panels in cabinetry doors

DIMENSIONS
16 x 16

PRODUCTS USED
Cabinetry: Wood-Mode, Sonoma door-style
Countertops: Caesarstone, Lagos Blue perimeter
Sink(s): Franke stainless
Faucets: Blanco Precision
Dishwasher: Miele
Range: Wolf
Lighting: Tech
Refrigerator: Sub-Zero
Wallcovering: Dunn Edwards paint
Warming drawer: Dacor
Steamer: Gaggenau
Coffee maker: Miele
Microwave: Sharp

MEMBER OF
SEN DESIGN GROUP

PHOTOGRAPHER: STEVEN PAUL WHITSITT

Function and Flair

A FREQUENT ENTERTAINER of family and friends, this Massachusetts homeowner felt that his existing culinary/dining array was too tight on space. The spatial deficit also prevented the client from displaying his antique furnishings and other treasured collectibles. Ready for a redo, this homeowner challenged Cathy and Ed of Renovisions, inc. with the task of reimagining the room.

To dramatically open the area, the design skills of Renovisions, along with the contracting skills of the homeowner and his brother, merged the kitchen and dining room, adding extra square footage at the rear of the home. To ensure that nary an inch of space went to waste, Renovisions created a uniquely shaped custom radius island. The piece showcases stunning two-tier contrasting-quartz countertops, which warm up the room.

Other functional features include deep drawers, a recessed Fisher & Paykel dish drawer, prep sink, pull-out trash bin, custom wine rack, and cabinetry to store bar supplies. The Victorian-style cherry cabinets with beaded details blend impeccably with the homeowner's antique furniture. Furthering the airy aesthetic, dazzling glass mullion doors along the entire length of the kitchen sink wall reflect the beautiful collectibles the homeowner now proudly displays. After a long day's work, the client now can come home to relax and feel like the king of his newly built castle! «

DESIGNER
Catherine M. Follett
Renovisions, inc.
150 Broadway
Hanover, MA 02339
781.826.0559

SPECIAL FEATURES
Tler countertop on island with custom curved radius, custom built-in wine rack on island and hanging above island, recessed dish drawer, custom mullion wall cabinets

DIMENSIONS
19 x 21

PRODUCTS USED
Cabinetry: Dura Supreme Victoria Panel in Wild Cherry finish
Countertops: Silestone Quartz "Nile"
Sink(s): Artisan stainless
Faucets: Gerber
Refrigerator: GE
Cooktop: GE Profile
Oven: GE Profile
Dishwasher: Bosch
Lighting: Recessed, undercabinet
Other: U-Line wine refrigerator

MEMBER OF
SEN DESIGN GROUP

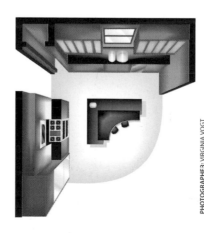

PHOTOGRAPHER: VIRGINIA VOGT

Pretty in Pembroke

PRETTY IS EXACTLY what the homeowners dreamed for during the nearly eight years they spent planning their kitchen renovation. Their appliances were outdated and tired, including the two-burner cooktop on their tile island countertop, which was not adequate for their family. They contacted Cathy and Ed of Renovisions, inc. to help create a design for a more functional, well-lit, better organized workspace with more storage options for their family.

The challenge: to include each feature the homeowner desired after moving the peninsula over to make room for their new 54-inch round table. The stainless steel dual-fuel range, smart dispense dishwasher and a stainless steel farmer's sink were at the top of the homeowners' list. A two-sided appliance garage, deep-wide drawers and large pantry cabinets with pullouts added storage. A wine rack showcasing their favorite spirits is an especially eye-catching feature.

Renovisions boxed out a new window overlooking the beautiful backyard, with a matching granite sill to accommodate a small herb garden the homeowners always envisioned. The various forms of lighting include recessed, pendant, undercabinet task and interior glass cabinet lighting and evoke a warm, inviting ambiance. From concept to completion, these homeowners were thrilled with their new Renovision and have been cooking up a storm ever since! «

DESIGNER
Catherine M. Follett
Renovisions, inc.
150 Broadway
Hanover, MA 02339
781.826.0559

SPECIAL FEATURES
Two-sided corner cabinet with glass doors and appliance garage; custom tile backsplash; undercabinet outlet strips; boxed-out window with matching peacock green granite sill; undercabinet and interior cabinet lighting

DIMENSIONS
28 x 16

PRODUCTS USED
Cabinetry: Dura Supreme, maple ginger
Flooring: Hardwood, oak
Countertops: Granite, peacock green
Sink(s): Elkay, stainless steel, farmer's
Faucets: Danze
Dishwasher: GE Profile
Refrigerator: GE Profile
Wallcovering: Paint, Martin Senour
Oven: GE Profile
Microhood: GE Profile
Hardware: Top Knobs

MEMBER OF

SEN DESIGN GROUP

PHOTOGRAPHER: TOM MALAMES

Passing Through

WHEN THESE HANOVER, MASS. homeowners contacted Cathy Follett and Ed Spooner of Renovisions, inc. to discuss their new kitchen, they quickly realized that with the three-month deadline of their daughter's graduation party, there was no time to waste. The designers presented a design to maximize storage by using a lazy Susan, deep pot and pan drawers, a pull-out spice rack, a pull-out double trash bin and a countertop appliance garage for storage of snacks that would otherwise clutter the counter.

The design also accomplished the homeowners' desire to create a more open feel in the adjacent dining room by replacing the partition wall with a steel beam and peninsula cabinets with access from both sides. The pass-through design gave the homeowners the openness they wanted, without sacrificing much cabinet space. The soffit used to encase the beam is carried throughout the rest of the kitchen. Cathy & Ed installed glass door cabinets in the middle section to provide the homeowners with a place to store and display their fine Italian dishes. Basket-weave glass, a glass shelf and the glow of interior halogen lights all help create the desired ambiance. The final design brings about an open, elegant layout, accomplishing the clients' goals to the very detail. «

DESIGNER
Catherine M. Follett
Renovisions, inc.
150 Broadway
Hanover, MA 02339
781.826.0559

SPECIAL FEATURES
Pass-through with access from both sides; basket-weave glass doors with interior lighting; entertainment bar/sink area

DIMENSIONS
16 x 26

PRODUCTS USED
Cabinetry: Dura Supreme
Flooring: Amtico Grey Onyx Designer
Countertops: Sensa Granite in Paradiso Bausch
Sink(s): Kindred, Whitehaus
Faucet(s): Danze
Oven: GE Profile
Microwave: GE Profile
Hardware: Top Knobs
Glass: Whittemore-Durgin, Larry's Glass

MEMBER OF
SEN DESIGN GROUP

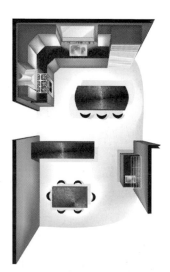

PHOTOGRAPHER: LEROY

Wine and Dine

A TRUE GEM and picturesque getaway, this weekend retreat in the Napa Valley is actually a second home to a San Francisco-based couple. With an abundance of vineyard views with horses from every window, this is country living at its best.

This fabulous kitchen was designed by Catherine Shackford of North Bay Kitchen and Bath, also in Napa. Shackford has more than 19 years' experience in kitchen design, and this kitchen is one she says she will never forget. The original space featured six pantries, oversized cabinets, and extra high ceilings. To accentuate the lofty verticality, Shackford designed floor-to-ceiling cabinetry with backlit glass upper doors, which kept the look light and airy and added a wonderful ambiance.

She consulted with the owners to install a wine bar to replace one of their many pantries, and they loved the idea. The piece really accentuates the couple's lifestyle: They not only love to entertain, but they also produce their own wine. The designer used glass in all the upper cabinets in the wine bar, giving the area a hutch-like appearance. To accommodate the homeowners' request, a built-in coffee machine was installed to the left of the sink, and a built-in garbage dispenser was installed below to catch the drippings.

The result is a space that exudes a sense of relaxation and warmth and is bar none the perfect place for entertaining. «

DESIGNER
Catherine Shackford
North Bay Kitchen
and Bath
1916 Yajome St.
Napa, CA 94559
707.224.1020

SPECIAL FEATURES
Wine bar with large wine cooler

DIMENSIONS
19 x 12

PRODUCTS USED
Cabinetry: Dura Supreme Country Traditions
Countertops: Mocha concrete
Sink(s): Rohl apron-front for main, Native Trails for wine bar
Faucets: Rohl
Refrigerator: GE Monogram
Cooktop: Thermador gas
Oven: Dacor
Warming Drawer: Dacor
Wine Cooler: Sub-Zero
Dishwasher: ASKO
Coffee Maker: Dacor built-in
Backsplash: Travertine in Light Walnut
Hardware: Top Knobs

MEMBER OF
SEN DESIGN GROUP

PHOTOGRAPHER: DONA BONICK

Elegant Simplicity

THESE HOMEOWNERS DECIDED to build their dream home in the hills of the Napa Valley Wine Country, and Catherine Shackford at North Bay Kitchen & Bath was chosen to bring their kitchen to life.

This couple had already decided on their Verde St. Denis marble long before coming into the showroom, so the Dura Supreme cabinets were chosen to serve as the perfect match. A burgundy stain was a stunning complement to the spectacular movement in the marble.

The homeowners also requested seating for four at the island, and after working on a design for several days, the T-shaped island was devised. An Olivieri prep sink is in the perfect location for convenient vegetable cleaning before heading off to cook it on the rangetop.

Each of the GE Monogram appliances was strategically placed to obtain the best possible work space. A niche for the TV is a great place to catch the news with a cup of coffee.

The angled dishwasher was a bit of a challenge, but by sinking it slightly into the wall, the desired angle was achieved. A stainless steel backsplash and Brazilian cherry wood flooring finished off the design. In the end, the kitchen had the perfect layout for entertaining friends and family. «

DESIGNER

Catherine Shackford
North Bay Kitchen & Bath
1916 Yajome St.
Napa, CA 94559
707.224.1020

SPECIAL FEATURES

Stainless steel backsplash; cookbook shelves in T-shaped island; corner dishwasher

DIMENSIONS

12 x 15

PRODUCTS USED

Cabinetry: Dura Supreme
Flooring: Brazilian Cherry wood
Countertops: Verde St. Denis marble
Sink(s): Oliveri, main and prep
Faucets: Hansgrohe
Dishwasher: GE Monogram
Lighting: Can and pendent lighting
Refrigerator: GE
Wallcovering: Paint
Oven/microwave: GE
Hood: GE stainless steel

MEMBER OF

SEN DESIGN GROUP

Fantasy Island

THE OWNERS OF THIS hilltop home selected Northbay Kitchen & Bath to remodel their kitchen. This offered many challenges for the designer and builder, David Frym, and his team. After completely gutting their galley kitchen, Frym added new electrical and plumbing and an enlarged window, maximizing the property's view.

The homeowners desired a large center island to act as a workspace and storage area with seating. The wood countertop serves as a handy work surface, as well as provides a contrast to the granite countertops throughout the kitchen. The island cabinets and bookcase in distressed white finish are a sharp contrast to the dark exotic lyptus woods of the kitchen and desk area. The shuttered doors and detailed trim and molding create an island atmosphere. And the stone and glass backsplash provides a luxurious backdrop to the custom-made copper hood above the range.

Ample storage fills the room, where glass-paneled and shuttered cabinetry highlights the design. The island is the ideal gathering spot for family and entertaining friends for special occasions. The kitchen expands to a cozy seating area with a fireplace and new large sliding doors connecting the deck and the lush backyard. «

DESIGNER
David Frym
Northbay Kitchen & Bath
822 Petaluma Blvd. N.
Petaluma, CA 94952
707.769.1646

SPECIAL FEATURES
Multipurpose island with bookcases and built-in desk area; custom Rangecraft copper hood; Speckva wood island countertop

DIMENSIONS
14' x 17'

PRODUCTS USED
Cabinetry: Dura Supreme, lyptus
Flooring: Oak with ebony finish
Countertops: Granite, island Speckva
Faucets: Perrin & Rowe; Rohl
Sinks: Rohl
Dishwasher: KitchenAid
Range: Wolf
Oven: Wolf
Lighting: Recessed; ambience undercabinet; pendants
Refrigerator: Sub-Zero
Wallcovering: Benjamin Moore paint
Microwave: KitchenAid
Wine cooler: KitchenAid
Hood: Rangecraft custom

MEMBER OF
SEN DESIGN GROUP

PHOTOGRAPHER: STEVEN PAUL WHITSITT

Sparing No Expense

WHEN HOMEOWNERS KEN AND BRENDA decided to build their dream home in the heart of the wine country, they spared no expense. To make their dreams a reality, the homeowners turned to Ken Roberts, a general contractor in Sonoma County. Roberts, in turn, sought the kitchen design expertise of his friend and fellow contractor, David Frym, owner of D & R Construction and Northbay Kitchen & Bath. Together, Roberts and Frym sought out the ideal components for the residence, including a trip to the Kitchen & Bath Industry show in Las Vegas.

Since entertainment and comfort were paramount, Roberts and Frym created a culinary space with an open floor plan that flows into the adjacent expansive family room. The kitchen cabinetry consists of Encore Fine Cabinetry's best line, complete with hand-carved details and glass–paneled upper cabinets.

Inside the family room, a tiled fireplace crowned by a custom mantel mirrors the kitchen cabinetry. This space also extends into the dining/living room areas, where the ceiling opens to a multilevel height, and the floors consist of hand-scraped hickory plank. Every detail throughout the space exudes an elegant yet casual ambiance. The result is a home conducive to delightful entertaining and dining with friends and family. «

DESIGNER

David Frym
Northbay Kitchen & Bath
822 Petaluma Blvd. N.
Petaluma, CA 94952
707.769.1646

SPECIAL FEATURES

Hand-scraped hickory plank floors; hand-painted tile backsplash; hand-carved cabinet corbels, details; apron-front sink

DIMENSIONS

17 x 18

PRODUCTS USED

Cabinetry: Encore Fine Cabinetry
Flooring: Travertine tile
Countertops: Limestone slab
Sink(s): Rohl
Faucets: Rohl
Dishwasher: KitchenAid
Cooktop: Viking
Lighting: Recessed Ambiance undercabinet
Refrigerator: KitchenAid
Wallcovering: Benjamin Moore Warm Tones
Oven: Viking
Hardware: Top Knobs
Backsplash: Tilevera

MEMBER OF

SEN DESIGN GROUP

PHOTOGRAPHER: STEVEN PAUL WHITSITT

Spanish Hacienda

THE OWNERS OF THIS HOME WANTED TO TRANSFORM THEIR MODEST, ranch-style house into a warm and inviting Spanish hacienda suitable for family living and entertaining. The home sits nestled on a mature hillside. The property allowed for the home's expansion, but due to preexisting elements, it did pose some design challenges. To achieve their desired space, the clients consulted with Sandra T. Rodriguez, CKD, who creatively designed a new addition.

The original kitchen, nook and dining room were small and cramped. As a result, the homeowners wanted their new living area to be roomy and have a cohesive flow. The new addition is an 18' x 20' dynamic space with angled walls. An outdated exterior mechanical room was utilized and converted into an underground interior wine cellar. The original outside staircase now leads directly from the kitchen down into the completed wine cellar. A custom-designed wrought iron gate was created to add ambiance and to function as a safety device for the couple's two young sons. A computer desk was worked into the space for family members to utilize while meals are being prepared. Ample counter space and the large island allow the client sufficient room for food preparation and buffet-style entertaining.

The new space is well integrated. The old kitchen nook became the new dining room, and the old dining room became the new entry. The mixture of color, textures and surfaces including cement, granite and tile countertops, along with faux-finished walls and custom-designed wrought iron fixtures accomplish the Old World, rustic atmosphere the homeowners dreamed of.

DESIGNER:
Sandra T. Rodriguez, CKD
L & S Interiors
1130 North Kraemer
Blvd., Suite D
Anaheim, CA 92806
714.998.8477

SPECIAL FEATURES:
Angled walls, integrated textured surfaces, hand-painted Mexican tile backsplash, wrought iron fixtures, multi-level counter on island

DIMENSIONS:
18 x 20

PRODUCTS USED:
Cabinetry: Merit Kitchens
Flooring: Satillo Mexican Pavers
Countertop: Custom-designed cement; Island/desk, Blue Fantasy granite
Sink(s): Whitehaus Fireclay farm sink; Island, Blanco stainless steel sink; Bar, Belle Foret copper sink
Faucets: Rohl
Dishwasher: Fisher Paykel dish drawers
Warming Drawer: Dacor 27"
Microwave: GE
Refrigerator: Sub-Zero
Wallcovering: Aged plaster faux painted
Range: Dacor
Hood: Modern-Aire Pro Hood Liner
Light fixtures, bakers rack, wine cellar gate: Art Manufactures, Inc.

PHOTOGRAPHER: STEVEN PAUL WHITSITT

Contempo Cucina

IN THE MIDST of an entire home remodel, Kitchen & Bath Design Consultants (KBDC) designed this incredible kitchen to meet the needs and expectations of these Connecticut homeowners. The formal dining room, family room and kitchen were merged into one large space, supporting European-style cabinets, stainless steel appliances, stone countertops and exquisite applications of glass and porcelain tile.

The room is of remarkable style and sleekness. The crisp and clean earth tone colors, lighting and design provide a stunning ambiance. A multilevel countertop makes perfect use of space by doubling the workspace. Dark cabinetry is highlighted by contemporary hardware, which ties into the stainless appliances throughout the room. The central island, loaded with ample storage, holds the weight of the room and creates space enough for everyone to gather around while meals are prepared.

The colonial-style home was modernized inside and out while maintaining its luxurious and timeless milieu, pleasing the homeowners and the designers of KBDC. Every window was replaced, the roof redone, heating system updated and the entire first floor was gutted and rebuilt, all while the homeowners remained living within. The updating of the home was a total success and the results are breathtaking. «

DESIGNER
Lorey Cavanaugh CKD, CBD and Design Team
Kitchen & Bath Design Consultants LLC
1000 Farmington Ave.
West Hartford, CT 06107
860.232.2872

Kitchen & Bath Design Consultants of Bantam
828 Bantam Road
Bantam, CT 06750
860.567.9229

SPECIAL FEATURES
Raised bar on aluminum supports on island; incorporation of new structural steel and glass backsplash for the island cooktop/hood; glass mosaic backsplash; multiple countertop materials

DIMENSIONS
12 x 14

PRODUCTS USED
Cabinetry: UltraCraft upper cabinets, Destiny, aluminum wall cabinets
Flooring: Strip maple, natural finish
Countertops: Upper counter in Black Marinace, lower counter in CaesarStone-honed finish
Sink(s): Kindred Crown
Faucet(s): Blanco
Dishwasher: Bosch
Cooktop: Wolf
Lighting: Resolute
Refrigerator: Sub-Zero
Backsplash: MLW Stone
Double oven: Viking
Hood: Zephyr Milano glass
Microwave: GE
Disposal: Waste King

MEMBER OF

SEN DESIGN GROUP

PHOTOGRAPHER: OLSON PHOTOGRAPHIC LLC

Kosher Style

THIS KITCHEN IS a perfect example of form following function, kosher style. When this family decided to remodel, they created an extensive wish list. In their search for the perfect firm, the homeowners stopped at Küche+Cucina in Paramus, New Jersey.

Also challenging were the family's many requirements, among them the desire for an attractive, comfortable space for casual dining and family gatherings with a contemporary flair. The kitchen also needed to be conducive to daily meal preparation and had to be kid-friendly. Finally, the space needed to be kosher—three sinks, two dishwashers, two ovens.

Küche+Cucina constructed a large center island to provide ample space for meal preparation; the lower tier is a perfect spot for the kids to do their school work. CaesarStone counters provide a beautiful nonporous, maintenance-free surface, ideal for a kosher kitchen. Three sinks allow for two simultaneous cooks. The pantries were lowered to create a "furniture" appearance while tying the kitchen to the dining room. When the design team finished their preparations, the homeowners' builder stepped in and prepared the space for the new kitchen. After the cabinets arrived from Italy, Küche+Cucina's installers fitted them. The countertops and sinks followed, and the new kitchen was ready for its first meal. «

DESIGNER
Küche+Cucina
489 Route 17 South
Paramus, NJ 07652
201.261.5221

268 Main St.
Madison, NJ 07940
973.937.6060

SPECIAL FEATURES
Kosher kitchen complete with two dishwashers, two ovens, three sinks; multilevel counter on island

DIMENSIONS
21 x 28

PRODUCTS USED
Cabinetry: Pedini, Borda in cherry
Flooring: Amtico
Countertops: CaesarStone
Sinks: Franke
Dishwasher: Miele, KitchenAid
Cooktop: DCS
Refrigerator: Sub-Zero
Oven: Miele, Wolf
Hood: Miele

MEMBER OF
SEN DESIGN GROUP

PHOTOGRAPHER: PETER RYMWID

Grand Comfort

WHEN THIS RIDGEWOOD, N.J., couple decided to renovate their kitchen, they came straight to Paramus-based Küche+Cucina, the same design firm that created the couple's first kitchen in their previous home. The homeowners' desire for the culinary space was a grand, but comfortable look. To accomplish this task, designer Amir Ilin worked closely with the homeowner, who knew exactly what she wanted.

To create their desired design, Ilin utilized elegant, hand-painted cabinetry. The cabinetry features many such intricate details as fluted columns and pilasters with rosettes, dentil crown moulding, carved wood corbels and furniture bases. Four separate work sections add much-needed function to the room, and the fully integrated refrigerator blends in seamlessly with the cabinetry. White carerra honed marble composes the countertops and backsplash, and a French La Cornue range tops off the space. The shelf above the range provides the perfect area to display a plate collection. The rug in front of the range ties the room together in perfect harmony, picking up the hues in the wallpaper. In the end, appreciates the fabulous design of this functional East Coast kitchen. «

DESIGNER
Amir Ilin
Küche+Cucina
489 Route 17 S.
Paramus, NJ 07652
201.261.5221

268 Main Street
Madison, NJ 07940
973.937.6060

SPECIAL FEATURES
Fully-integrated refrigerators; French La Cornue Range

DIMENSIONS
16.5 x 20

PRODUCTS USED
Cabinetry: Küche+Cucina handcrafted
Flooring: Wood
Countertops: White carerra honed marble
Sink(s): Rohl
Faucet(s): Rohl
Dishwasher: Miele
Refrigerator: Sub-Zero
Oven: LaCornue
Wallcovering: Wallpaper

MEMBER OF
SEN DESIGN GROUP

PHOTOGRAPHER: PETER RYMWID

A Family Affair

As hazelnuts roast in the oven, three generations of women prepare the ingredients for the night's dinner. The men discuss business, while the children watch television, all waiting impatiently to enjoy great-grandmother's signature dish. Sound like a holiday gathering? Hardly. This generational gathering is an everyday event in this kitchen space, the heart of a home that houses four family generations, ranging in age from 8 to 89 years old.

It's a difficult task for a designer to create a dream kitchen for one cook. Designing for three is quite another challenge. Nonetheless, Küche + Cucina dutifully tackled the task. The homeowners also hired interior decorator Joye Wesler, who worked closely with kitchen designer Gina M. Ko to create this dream kitchen for the family.

The area demanded maximum efficiency and ultimate comfort. Careful consideration was given to the physical limitations of the great-grandmother. Designers eliminated or softened hard corners without sacrificing design, and the round island solved the major issues. Curved cabinets help the second cook work more efficiently and create additional visibility necessary for keeping an eye out for elders and children. A cozy eating area promotes interaction among the family members. «

DESIGNER:
Gina Myong Ko
Küche + Cucina
489 Route 17 South
Paramus, NJ 07652
201.261.5221

SPECIAL FEATURES:
Two work triangles; multi-level glass counters on round island

DIMENSIONS:
22 x 21

PRODUCTS USED:
Cabinetry: Pedini Island; Neff
Countertops: Uba Tuba granite
Sinks: Franke
Dishwasher: Bosch
Cooktop: Viking & Wolf
Lighting: Custom lighting over island
Refrigerator: Sub-Zero
Oven: Thermador
Interior Decorator: Joye Wesler

MEMBER OF
SEN DESIGN GROUP

PHOTOGRAPHER: PETER RYMWID

Winning Recipe

THE HOMEOWNERS OF THIS NEW JERSEY HOME hungered for a larger layout for their cramped kitchen, which, besides its lack of square footage, was seriously short on storage. So when it came time to remodel, the couple entrusted Bernard Kim with Küche+Cucina to put a new face on their time-worn space.

After consulting with his clients, Kim pressed forward with the project, paying close attention to their request for an ultra-modern kitchen with copious storage space, a blunt corner, a stack of cabinets and a strategically placed spot for the refrigerator. To meet their objectives, the designer knocked out walls to open the room, effectively extending the space and adding an expansive feel. Upon Kim's recommendation, the homeowners opted for the use of contrasting color, which resulted in a stunning interplay of light and warmth. The blue-hued backsplash further enhances this artful aesthetic and lends a calming touch.

Though he had to contend with the room's many angles and a bank of cabinets that was challenging to lay out, Kim made quick work of the project, optimizing every opportunity to make the kitchen shine. While space may have been at a premium in the original room, this culinary creation satiated all of the homeowners' requests. «

DESIGNER
Bernard Kim
Küche+Cucina
489 Rt. 17 South
Paramus, NJ 07652
201.261.5221

SPECIAL FEATURES
Built-in open cabinet into wall; glass cabinet for china display; 4-inch stainless steel countertop with aluminum accent

DIMENSIONS
12 x 18

PRODUCTS USED
Cabinetry: Pedini, dark oak
Flooring: Concrete
Countertops: CaesarStone, Blizzard
Sink(s): Franke
Faucet(s): Franke
Dishwasher: Miele
Cooktop: Miele
Oven: Miele
Lighting: Halogen hanging pendant
Refrigerator: Sub-Zero
Wallcovering: Paint
Microwave: GE Profile
Backsplash: Glass

MEMBER OF
SEN DESIGN GROUP

PHOTOGRAPHER: PETER RYMWID

Creative Corbels

THE DESIGN CREATIVITY of Küche+Cucina's Amir Ilin and Bernard Kim shines again in this lovely New Jersey home, located in a historic preservation area. The team from South Orange, N.J., expertly attained their goal of maintaining the original feeling while also incorporating moods of creativity and comfort.

The clients wanted the room to feature large pilaster legs, but they did not want them to take too much of the kitchen's space. As a result, Ilin and Kim suggested and created a pull-out spice rack to provide functionality within the superb design detail.

The kitchen features six pull-out pilasters, meeting the desires of the clients and earning absolute eye appeal. They also put their design finesse to work by creating custom corbels. A custom-built hood canopy gives an elegant focal point, while custom-shaped corbels carry out the theme of the room. The mantel coordinates with the room, tying together design in perfect harmony. The perfect place to display the homeowner's collection of dishware, it adds unique personality to the space. The kitchen is filled with an airy ambiance and the strategically placed lighting mixes with the natural sunlight, which pours in through the window. The finished design exudes elegance, while providing complete usability. «

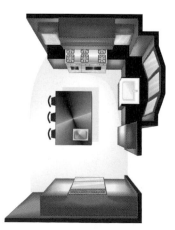

DESIGNER
Amir Ilin and
Bernard Kim
Küche+Cucina
489 Route 17 South
Paramus, NJ 07652
201.261.5221

SPECIAL FEATURES
Pull-outs hidden
behind the four pilaster
columns; custom-built
canopy; custom-shaped
corbel

DIMENSIONS
20 x 25

PRODUCTS USED
Cabinetry: Küche+Cucina
handcrafted cabinetry
Flooring: Porcelain tile
Countertops: Cashmere
Gold Granite
Sink(s): Rohl
Faucet(s): Rohl
Dishwasher: Fisher &
Paykel
Range: Wolf
Refrigerator: Sub-Zero
Wallcovering: Paint
Microwave: Wolf
Coffee machine: Miele
Warming drawer: Miele

MEMBER OF
SEN DESIGN GROUP

PHOTOGRAPHER: PETER RYMWID

Old World Design

THIS MASTERPIECE KITCHEN IS PART of a Saddle River, New Jersey, family's dream home. Given that the homeowners already owned a number of beautiful homes, they were experienced in making design decisions. For this project, they chose a French country design.

At the recommendation of their builder, the homeowners met with Amir Ilin, owner of Küche+Cucina, Paramus. Upon visiting the showroom and meeting Ilin, the homeowners hired him for the project. Ilin collaborated with the designer, Barbara Ostrom of Barbara Ostrom Associates to create the finished project.

This active family uses their kitchen often for meals and gatherings, as well as for large dinner parties. The 1,200-square-foot space required considerable creativity to make it attractive and functional. The biggest design challenge was the home's shape. By strategically placing three different-shaped islands in three different finishes, Ilin and Ostrom were able to turn the space into a functional, working kitchen. The different colors were carried throughout the room in the cabinetry, the tile behind the range and in the ceiling's inserts.

Ilin and Ostrom used a variety of textures, finishes and shapes to create an atmosphere of old world charm with functional, modern conveniences. «

DESIGNER
Amir Ilin
Küche+Cucina
489 Rt. 17 South
Paramus, NJ 07652
201.261.5221

SPECIAL FEATURES
Three islands; two face-to-face refrigerators integrated into a cabinet resembling a French armoire; five cabinet finishes; coffered ceilings with special relief inserts and handmade tile inserts; limestone finish hood

DIMENSIONS
42 x 28

PRODUCTS USED
Cabinetry: Küche+Cucina handcrafted cabinetry
Flooring: Jerusalem Stone in a four-piece pattern
Countertops: Jerusalem Stone, Oro Castello granite, Spekva cherry wood top
Sink(s): Herbeau, Franke
Faucets: Rohl
Dishwasher: KitchenAid (2)
Refrigerator: Sub-Zero (4)
Wallcovering: Faux painting
Range: Viking

MEMBER OF
SEN DESIGN GROUP

PHOTOGRAPHER: PHILLIP ENNIS

Entertaining Oasis

THE OWNER OF this Madison, Wisconsin, home desired a roomy epicurean space that would incorporate an open floor plan and would complement the rest of the main-floor living area. The homeowner also desired a design to provide ample space for weekend gatherings of college students and their parents while maintaining a warm close-knit, comfortable abode during the remainder of the week.

To achieve this, the team at Bella Domicile created a separate holding kitchen complete with sink, refrigerator and warming drawer for use by caterers during any social event. The implementation of a separate holding area frees up valuable countertop space and creates an open environment suitable for entertaining guests and visitors without creating a sense of being crowded. The main kitchen features an attractive island in three distinct heights ideal for the placement of dishes, hors d' oeuvres trays and other serving dishes. Appliances including a wine storage system, ice maker, microwave pull-out drawer and built-in coffee maker support and enhance any entertainment needs. Now whether entertaining large gatherings or preparing a quiet meal for two, the homeowners delight in this attractive kitchen, which inspires and stirs the senses and creates an oasis from the rest of the world. «

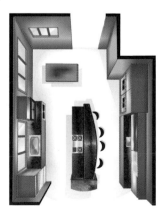

DESIGNER
Bella Domicile
Design Team
Bella Domicile Inc.
6210 Nesbitt Road
Madison, WI 53719
608.271.8241

SPECIAL FEATURES
Separate holding kitchen for caterers; multilevel countertops; two-tone wood finishes on cabinetry; secondary trough sink

DIMENSIONS
17 x 16

PRODUCTS USED
Cabinetry: Dura Supreme Designer Series
Flooring: Tile
Countertops: Natural stone, wood
Dishwasher: Asko
Cooktop: Wolf
Refrigerator: Sub-Zero
Oven: Wolf
Microwave drawer: Sharp
Coffeemaker: Miele
Sink(s): Kohler

MEMBER OF
SEN DESIGN GROUP

PHOTOGRAPHER: MIKE REBHOLZ

Twice as Nice

The challenge involved with this project was to take an 18-year-old kitchen originally crafted by the designer, Allen Curran CKD of Bella Domicile Inc., and reinvent that space for the same homeowners. The previous kitchen incorporated a contemporary feel, but the homeowners' new desire was for a richer and warmer space with more detail and interest.

The general floor plan worked well; however, the owners wanted to draw guests further into the room instead of seating them at a round table at one end of the kitchen. Curran accomplished this by installing a raised snack bar at one end of the island with rounded seating, which tapers off along the backside of the island.

The next phase of design was to add warmth and detail. The focus: a more intriguing mantel hood, which then expanded to a decorative wood beamed ceiling, featuring two different woods and horizontal glass tile. The pair of materials—maple with a natural finish to match the reused wood floor and cherry with a chestnut coating—adds contrast to the space.

Marked by a thorough and consistent attention to detail, the design is highlighted by the horizontal detail of natural maple on both the backside of the island, island legs and the canopy hood and the edges of the beams in the ceiling. «

DESIGNER
Allen Curran CKD, WRID
Bella Domicile Inc.
6210 Nesbitt Road
Madison, WI 53719
608-271-8241

SPECIAL FEATURES
Raised snack bar; mantel hood; furniture leg detail

DIMENSIONS
22 x 17

PRODUCTS USED
Cabinetry: Dura Supreme
Flooring: Maple
Countertops: Natural stone
Sink(s): Undermount
Dishwasher: Asko
Cooktop: Wolf
Oven: GE
Refrigerator: Sub-Zero
Warming drawer: GE

MEMBER OF
SEN DESIGN GROUP

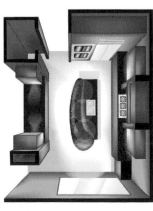

PHOTOGRAPHER: STEVEN PAUL WHITSITT

Flying High

WHEN THIS MADISON, WISCONSIN, homeowner decided he wanted to update his kitchen, he knew he wanted something that was definitely out of the ordinary yet a representation of his style. To turn his vision into reality, he turned to Garrett Dynes, a designer at Bella Domicile Inc.

First, the wall between the small kitchen and dining room was removed to open up the kitchen. The homeowner entertains often, so the removal of one wall quickly turned into removing three, creating today's popular open floor plan.

Black quartz was used as a contrast to the warm natural beech cabinetry. A trough sink for beverages was incorporated into the back side of the island. The faucet was placed where it can double as a pot filler for the island's cooktop, and a distinctive light fixture was selected to highlight this unique sink feature.

To the right of the oversized triple-bowl sink are aluminum and frosted-glass accent cabinets. Born from these staggered cabinets is this kitchen's signature feature: a custom-designed flyover that organically moves across the ceiling, effectively breaking up this now large ceiling plane.

With some of the gatherings going well into the evening, the backlit flyover—and other unique details—really gives this homeowner and his guests the feeling they're in a trendy downtown lounge versus a kitchen. «

DESIGNER
Garrett Dynes
Bella Domicile Inc.
6210 Nesbitt Road
Madison, WI 53719
608.271.8241

SPECIAL FEATURES
Raised trough sink top, flyover, aluminum and frosted-glass accent cabinets

DIMENSIONS
23 x 14

PRODUCTS USED
Cabinetry: Custom Cupboards in Natural Beech
Flooring: Porcelain tile
Countertops: Zodiaq
Sink(s): Kohler
Cooktop: Dacor
Oven: Dacor
Refrigerator: KitchenAid
Dishwasher: Frigidaire

MEMBER OF
SEN DESIGN GROUP

PHOTOGRAPHER: MARCIA HANSEN

Lake Activity

THE OWNERS OF this beautiful lake home were concerned that the existing kitchen had no view of the water and that the rarely used dining room stole the show. The design solution Denise Quade, CKD of Bella Domicile Inc., came up with was to remove the wall between the spaces and merge the two areas. Also, because this couple often entertains, all of the openings to the adjacent rooms needed to be enlarged to provide a picture-perfect vantage point.

The highly personalized space was designed for an avid cook who loves to entertain, as well as for a busy family with four active kids from ages 10 to 18. A message center equipped with file drawers and organizers for everyday schedules helps the family stay on track. A flat screen television was perfectly sized to the open shelf and is situated within close view of the table and work areas in the kitchen. Two colors of cabinets were used throughout. Additionally, honed granite countertops were combined with a wenge wood countertop.

Preparation, cooking, cleanup and refrigeration were deliberately zoned. The wine refrigerator and ice maker were separated for easy entertaining. A second sink was located close to the bar area and food prep zone. The re-imagined kitchen is understated elegance—functional yet comfortable with a gorgeous lake view. «

DESIGNER
Denise Quade, CKD
Bella Domicile Inc.
6210 Nesbitt Road
Madison, WI 53719
608.271.8241

SPECIAL FEATURES
Two-tone cabinetry; honed granite countertops; wenge wood top; inset and full overlay door styles

DIMENSIONS
33 x 13

PRODUCTS USED
Cabinetry: Dura Supreme, Designer Series
Flooring: Wood
Countertops: Honed Geriba granite and wenge wood
Dishwasher: Asko
Range: Wolf
Refrigerator: Sub-Zero
Wine storage: Sub-Zero

MEMBER OF
SEN DESIGN GROUP

PHOTOGRAPHER: GREG SUTTER

Open Invitation

The owners of this Middleton, Wisconsin, dwelling dreamed of a larger kitchen that was more open and accessible to the rest of their residence. With their son's upcoming marriage and subsequent parties and gatherings planned at their home, the owners called on Traci Rauner of Bella Domicile to help transform their space in time for the big day.

Of their many requests, one of the most important was to make the dining and family rooms more visible from the kitchen. The owners also wanted to view the fireplace from the island. To meet their needs, Rauner removed the wall shared with the dining room to expand the space and to create the open plan the owners envisioned. Rauner also added cabinets to the rear of the peninsula to accommodate their numerous sets of silverware and dishes.

To further enhance the storage space, Rauner incorporated three large pantries, as well as extra-deep wall cabinets. She also took special care to separate the functions of the kitchen to allow for multiple cooks simultaneously—a big boon during the wedding breakfast when five people worked to make the meal. The result is a beautiful, functional space that fits dozens of guests with ease while providing a relaxing spot for the homeowners to enjoy even after the wedding bells have tolled. «

DESIGNER
Traci Rauner
Bella Domicile Inc.
6210 Nesbitt Road
Madison, WI 53719
608.271.8241

SPECIAL FEATURES
Lower-counter baking area; double-depth wine cubby storage; stacked cabinetry; TV behind pocket doors; painted black accent mouldings

DIMENSIONS
13 x 23

PRODUCTS USED
Cabinetry: Dura Supreme Designer Series, Napa door style, Maple/Butternut finish
Flooring: Wood
Countertops: Tropic Brown granite
Dishwasher: Asko
Cooktop: Wolf
Refrigerator: Sub-Zero
Wallcovering: Paint
Oven: Wolf
Microwave: Wolf convection
Undercounter refrigeration: Sub-Zero

MEMBER OF
SEN DESIGN GROUP

PHOTOGRAPHER: GREG SUTTER

A New Era

Built in 1918, this house had not changed owners until the current family purchased it in late 2005. The new owners wanted a larger kitchen with top-quality appliances that felt more open to the adjacent dining room but still kept the style of the house. They relied on their friend Joe Gelletich with Custom Crafters Inc. to help achieve their dream, which he had done in remodeling projects in their previous home and beach house.

The couple, both busy professionals, enjoy cooking and entertaining on their down time and wanted a kitchen to meet these needs. To create more space, Gelletich relocated the powder room to another area of the first floor. To connect the kitchen to the dining room, a pair of pocket doors with divided lights was added. A duo of French doors was also installed to bring in more light and create access to the large back porch and yard beyond. Enlarging the kitchen made space for an island that provided much needed storage, a work space and a place for friends and family to gather.

To keep with the style and era of the house, the client selected white painted cabinets with inset doors. Cork flooring, soapstone countertops and solid cherry on the island give this kitchen a warm feeling to satisfy the owners' preference for natural materials. The stainless steel appliances are top quality and make this kitchen a delight for a skilled cook to use. «

DESIGNER
Joseph W. Gelletich
Custom Crafters Inc.
4000 Howard Ave.
Kensington, MD 20895
301.493.4000

SPECIAL FEATURES
Soapstone farm sink;
cherry wood island
countertop; divided
light pocket doors;
divided light exterior
French doors

DIMENSIONS
12 x 16

PRODUCTS USED
Cabinetry: Dura Supreme
Designer Series
Flooring: Cork
Countertops: Soapstone
Sink(s): Soapstone farm
sink
Faucet(s): Grohe
Dishwasher: Bosch
Range: Wolf
Lighting: Lightolier
(recessed), Tech
(pendants)
Refrigerator: GE
Hood: Wolf

MEMBER OF
SEN DESIGN GROUP

PHOTOGRAPHER: STEVEN PAUL WHITSITT

Double the Assets

THIS HOME IN PERDIDO BEACH, ALABAMA, was in need of a fresh, new design. The homeowners, a couple with three small children, needed a space to accommodate everyone, as well as provide plenty of room to cook and entertain. To meet their design desires, the homeowners called upon Michael Davis and co-designer Trae Tittle of Coastal Kitchen & Bath, Inc., and the transformation began.

With proper, and extremely detailed, planning, the project didn't hit any snags along the way. To allow the cooks in the kitchen total functionality, a dual fuel cooking stove sits proudly in the space. Two full size dishwashers are the perfect complement, allowing large pots and pans to be cleaned, while the smaller items, like dishes and wine glasses, are washed separately.

This kitchen's special features make it a stand-out. It boasts a unique barrel ceiling in the kitchen area, a large island with two full-size dishwashers, and the most eye-catching feature, a pass-through beverage center off the kitchen with ice maker. In the end, the design was the perfect balance of a cooking space and social area, the ideal backdrop for this family's many gatherings. «

DESIGNER
Michael Davis
Trae Tittle, co-designer
Coastal Kitchen & Bath, Inc.
401 E. Riveria Blvd.
Foley, AL 36535
251.943.5258

SPECIAL FEATURES
Pine slat barrel ceiling with Chicago split brick floor

DIMENSIONS
27 X 25

PRODUCTS USED
Cabinetry: Shiloh
Flooring: Old Chicago split brick
Countertops: Granite, Brazil Black
Bartops: Granite, New Venetian Gold
Sink(s): J.S.I.
Faucets: Castille Collection
Dishwasher: KitchenAid Architect
Cooktop: KitchenAid Architect
Oven: KitchenAid Architect, double
Lighting: World Imports
Refrigerator: KitchenAid Architect
Wallcovering: Sherman Williams paint
Ice maker: KitchenAid Architect
Microwave: KitchenAid
Backsplash: Granite

MEMBER OF
SEN DESIGN GROUP

PHOTOGRAPHER: STEVE GORAUM

Savvy Storage

DESIGNED BY VALERY O. DOODY of Ellsworth Building Supply (EBS), this kitchen is the result of a post and beam barn remodel. Like many Maine islanders, the owners are a close-knit family and spend time entertaining during the winter. Thus they desired a warm, inviting space for family to gather. The goal: to design cabinets to surround the beams and columns while maintaining functionality. To usher in ample daylight, Doody arranged the cabinets and range to provide space for windows. Due to low ceilings, she customized the upper cabinets to a height of 27 inches and pushed the cabinetry toward the ceiling to provide much-needed storage. The designer also utilized a nook beneath the staircase for pantry space, and she concealed a three-bin cabinet behind an old sliding barn-style door. The cabinet holds pet food and recyclables.

Respecting the uncomplicated lines of the original building, Doody selected simple inset shaker cabinets and gray granite countertops. The black and white backsplash further enhances this color scheme. Additional functionality makes the kitchen user friendly: Cabinets flanking the range have pull-out spice racks, and most cabinets contain pull-out trays. A pull-up shelf provides a spot for the mixer and food processor. In the end, this storage-filled space more than pleased the homeowners. «

DESIGNER
Valery O. Doody
Ellsworth Building
Supply (EBS)
261 State St.
Ellsworth, ME 04605
207.667.7134

SPECIAL FEATURES
Custom hood over range with windows between; hidden storage behind sliding barn door

DIMENSIONS
20 x 10

PRODUCTS USED
Cabinetry: Hampshire
Flooring: Painted pine plank
Countertops: Granite
Sinks: Rohl, Franke
Faucets: Rohl, Franke
Range: AGA Legacy
Lighting: Progress under cabinets, recessed
Refrigerator: Maytag
Wallcovering: American Olean, Greenwich Village tile

MEMBER OF
SEN DESIGN GROUP

PHOTOGRAPHER: CHRIS PINCHBECK

Modern Luxury

THIS CALIFORNIA KITCHEN was in need of a total remodel—no simple face-lift would do. To get the area in shape and ready for the homeowners, Micky Yannay of Designer Kitchens LA planned the design with the utmost care and creativity.

The most daunting challenge in the existing traditional space was to transform it into a completely seamless modern design. The very contemporary look of the Pedini Italian cabinetry provided the perfect launching point. And the rest came together beautifully.

A bevy of storage solutions and a variety of accessories and hardware keep all utensils, whether large or small, in perfect order. High on storage, the space also is tall on stylish convenience, including its handsome Blumotion easy-gliding, self-closing drawers. The countertop material chosen was CaesarStone quartz—versus granite—because it is durable and non-porous. It's also scratch-, chemical-, crack-, stain- and heat-resistant, but still has the aesthetic beauty of granite.

The light-colored Travertine flooring offsets the dark cabinetry to create a dynamic look. The combination of gray glass, gray oak and white lacquered cabinetry provides a stunningly sleek look. Double ovens are the perfect addition to these homeowners' lifestyle, ideal for entertaining or an intimate meal for two. «

DESIGNER
Micky Yannay
Designer Kitchens LA
(Kitchen, Closet &
Bathroom Cabinetry)
23010 Ventura Blvd.
Woodland Hills, CA
91364
818.222.7405

SPECIAL FEATURES
Stainless steel accessories and hardware; self-closing drawers; vertical track-movable table extension; multilevel counter height; glossy lacquered lift-up doors

DIMENSIONS
33 x 23

PRODUCTS USED
Cabinetry: Pedini, gray oak with gray glass cabinets combined with glossy white lacquered lift-up doors
Flooring: Travertine
Countertops: CaesarStone
Sink(s): Blanco
Faucets: Dornbracht
Dishwasher: Gaggenau
Cooktop: Gaggenau
Refrigerator: Gaggenau
Oven: Gaggenau
Microwave: Miele
Hardware: Blum
Coffee machine: Miele
Backsplash: Glass

PHOTOGRAPHER: MICKY YANNAY

Old World Elegance

THIS HOME ON Prior Lake in Minnesota needed a stunning design to complement the lovely scenery while boasting an Old World European feel to match the home's features. To transform the space into an area of grace and comfort, Elaine Addison of Addison Interiors set to work.

The large family needed plenty of space to relax, as well as room to entertain if they decided to host a gathering. The backyard was a breathtaking venue for these get-togethers, especially during a beautiful sunset, so the kitchen needed to accommodate any occasion.

Adorned by a natural stone backsplash with metal-coated accents and a natural stone floor, the entire space exudes a soothing, organic feel. The main kitchen spigot features a pullout spray, and the prep sink uses a pull-down spray faucet. The pot filler with swing arm makes it a cinch for the chef to prep for meals.

The meticulous amount of detail that went into this space sets it apart from other designs, as seen in the cabinetry, staining, painting and stone, which surrounds the hood and the back of the range. The ceiling beams are painted and glazed, and the large island at center stage features a prep sink and bookshelf end. A custom black glaze Miele coffee bar provides the ideal way to wake up each day, and the double ovens and multiple dishwashers are the perfect appliances to manage a gathering. «

DESIGNER
Elaine Addison
Addison Interiors
3180 Country Road 42 West
Burnsville, MN 55337
952.746.9500

SPECIAL FEATURES
Center island with prep sink and bookshelf end; furniture-style custom cherry cabinets with glaze; custom black glaze Miele coffee bar

DIMENSIONS
28 x 17

PRODUCTS USED
Cabinetry: Custom cherry with glaze
Flooring: Natural stone
Countertops: Granite and rock split edge
Sink(s): Kohler, stainless steel, prep and main
Faucets: Kohler, main and prep; Grohe, pot filler
Dishwasher: Fisher & Paykel, two drawer and single door
Cooktop: Wolf
Refrigerator: Sub-Zero, custom doors
Wallcovering: Daplan
Oven: Wolf
Coffee maker: Miele
Soap dispenser: Kohler

Tuscan Triumph

A PART OF the original Arcady Estate of Montecito, this beautiful historic Tuscan villa was built around 1895. Much of the graceful structure remained intact; however, the kitchen underwent a remodel in the 1970s and, as a result, was dark, narrow and uninspired.

The new owners were determined to reinvent the kitchen and, in the process, develop an elegant culinary zone consistent with the vintage good looks throughout the rest of the home. Douglas Gheza with Gheza Group Design Studio was called in to meet this challenge.

The proportions of the space were extremely long and narrow and confined by a stairwell. To maximize space, Gheza and team tucked the refrigerator beneath the stairs. They then got to work completely reconfiguring the room, incorporating a small addition expanding the space and flooding it with natural light. WmOh's Custom Cabinetry was used, and the Tuscan door style was a perfect selection for this century-old villa. A wine storage center keeps reds and whites at the perfect temperature.

Warm, light colors, natural stone throughout and a beautiful beam detail in the ceiling combine to create the elegance that this grand home deserves. «

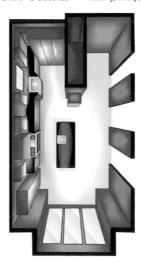

DESIGNER
Douglas Gheza, CID
Gheza Group Design Studio
532 Santa Barbara St.
Santa Barbara, CA 93101
805.899.2349

SPECIAL FEATURES
Furniture-style TV cabinet; furniture-style wine storage

DIMENSIONS
27 x 11

PRODUCTS USED
Cabinetry: WmOh's Handmade Cabinetry
Flooring: Beavillion Rubane French Limestone
Countertops: Granite
Sink(s): Stone Forest, copper, farm sink; Herbau, bar sink
Faucets: Harrington Brass, kitchen and bar
Dishwasher: Bosch
Range: Wolf
Refrigerator: Sub-Zero
Backsplash: Giallo, tumbled stone
Wine storage: Sub-Zero
Microwave: Thermador
Drawer pulls: Top Knobs, Tuscany, antique copper

Complete Treatment

THIS TWO-STORY GOLF course home was entirely remodeled. The first-floor kitchen walls and ceilings were removed at the studs. Overall, the original kitchen was not functional, as the rooms were compartmentalized and not conducive to entertaining.

The designer, Nancy Hugo CKD and Thomas DeFeo, DMD Design Builders, LLC, incorporated the support post into the design as well as the necessary heavy ceiling beams for the second floor. They reconfigured the total ceiling for the kitchen and dining area in a large, symmetrical grid. In order to give the newly expanded first floor the desired loft-like feel, Hugo and DeFeo, who have been working together for 10 years, designed a layout to maximize the spaciousness and impart a logical flow.

Since the kitchen can be viewed from the front door, it was important that simple lines and colors were used while still creating a memorable focal point. The chosen colors were soothing and contemporary and worked with the existing slate on the raised entry floor. The project turned out beautifully and could not have been completed without the other team members: Vicky Burton, VB Surfaces, tile contractor; Vern Mock, The Great Organization, custom cabinetry; Tom Tucker, Stone Counters of Arizona, countertop fabricator and Terry Wilfong of Best Home Appliances. «

DESIGN TEAM
Nancy Hugo CKD
602.469.6231

Thomas DeFeo
DMD Design Builders LLC
623.640.2416

SPECIAL FEATURES
One level island wrapping around second floor support post; two sinks in the island; white glazed subway tile; red pendants

DIMENSIONS
16 x 21

PRODUCTS USED
Cabinetry: Custom laminate, Pepperdust
Flooring: Patagonian Pecan engineered wood
Countertops: Silestone, Monte Blanc
Sinks: Lovello, undermount, stainless steel
Dishwasher: Bosch
Cooktop: GE
Lighting: Elk Pendants
Refrigerator: GE Monogram
Wallcovering: Frazee paint, Touchstone
Oven: GE
Microwave: Panasonic
Hood: Broan

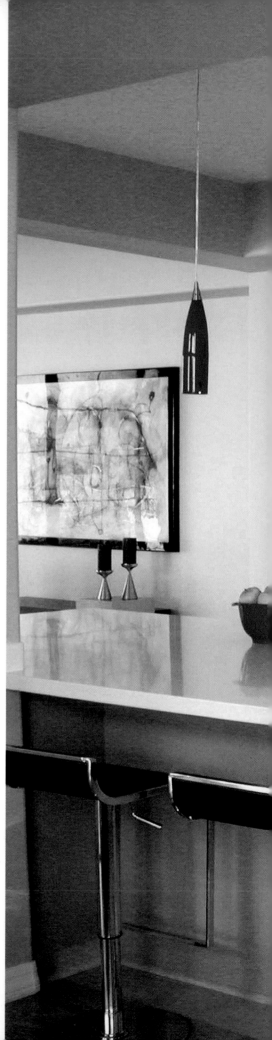

PHOTOGRAPHER: REALLYCOOL CONSULTING LLC

Dimensions of Design

THIS NEW CONSTRUCTION project built by Horizon Builders in Columbia, Missouri, needed to balance both function and aesthetics once the design was complete. The homeowners also enjoy entertaining, so the kitchen composition needed to be accommodating to friends and family.

With a ceiling height of nearly 12 feet, the room had plenty of space overhead but ran the risk of seeming too lofty and overwhelming. Fortunately, Malory Smith of Show Me Cabinets handled the design with finesse.

By installing 18 inches of crown molding and oversized cabinets, Smith created a sense of balance and proportion. She also incorporated large moldings in other parts of the room. Generously sized rope legs and ornate corbels in the bar area are perfectly proportioned additions to the airy space.

Two colors of stain on the cabinets give the room added contrast, and faux iron inserts in the open cabinets add stunning detail to the design. The hand-scraped hardwood provides a warm and inviting atmosphere, perfect for hosting a gathering. In the end, the room's abundant square footage was balanced with panache, providing a stylishly functional environment with design dimensions sure to please for years to come. «

DESIGNER
Malory Smith NCIDQ
Show Me Cabinets
1809 Nelwood
Columbia, MO 65202
573.256.2858

SPECIAL FEATURES
Oversized crown molding; faux iron door insets; large twisted-rope legs

DIMENSIONS
17 x 13

PRODUCTS USED
Cabinetry: Shiloh, knotty maple
Flooring: Hand-scraped hardwood
Countertops: Granite, golden beach
Sink(s): Stainless
Faucets: Moen
Dishwasher: GE
Cooktop: GE
Refrigerator: GE
Wallcovering: Faux paint
Oven: GE

PHOTOGRAPHER: BRAD NOBLITT

Warm and Bright

TWO YEARS AGO, this family of four bought a house nestled in the woods outside Chapel Hill, North Carolina. While the home boasted a cheerful and welcoming silhouette, the kitchen was congested, dark, and divided by walls. The dining room was also small, offering little opportunity for the homeowners to entertain, and the kitchen had no comfortable access into any other part of the house.

Bill Cederberg of Cederberg Kitchens & Additions got to know this family's everyday patterns. He took out a wall that separated the kitchen from the dining room and made the dining room part of the kitchen, highlighting the windows that lined the wall overlooking the backyard. Now, instead of looking out two small windows when they're standing at the sink, the family members can chat with friends across the bar while doing dishes or engaging in other culinary duties.

The kitchen and dining area are now bright, sunny, efficient, and inviting to large gatherings of friends or intimate family dinners. The kids can sit at the bar and eat breakfast and head right out the kitchen door, which was moved from the original, awkward location through the office. This family now lives in their kitchen, and it's made a world of difference! «

DESIGNER
Bill Cederberg
Cederberg Kitchens & Additions
630 Weaver Dairy Road, Suite 106
Chapel Hill, NC 27514
919.967.1171

SPECIAL FEATURES
Two islands: one two-level island with sink and a second island with undercounter beverage storage

DIMENSIONS
18 x 23

PRODUCTS USED
Cabinetry: Dura Supreme Crestwood with Arcadia CL door in knotty alder with Mission low-gloss finish
Flooring: Select red oak
Countertops: Uba Tuba granite
Sink(s): Grohe
Faucets: Grohe
Refrigerator: GE
Range: GE
Hood: Broan
Dishwasher: Bosch
Lighting: Task

MEMBER OF
SEN DESIGN GROUP

PHOTOGRAPHER: SETH TICE LEWIS

Natural Wonder

THIS KITCHEN IN CHAPEL HILL, North Carolina, needed a modern-day update from its 1970s contemporary style. To brighten up the room and create a more relaxed atmosphere that interacted with the wonderful natural vistas of the surrounding wooded slopes, William Cederberg of Cederberg Kitchens & Additions first removed a wall that isolated the kitchen from the dining room.

The floor plan expanded into an area originally created as a storage utility shed, and the team had to rework the electric panel and reposition the refrigerator to allow for a new set of tall pantry cabinets, which greatly increased storage.

A small peninsula now stands in place of the wall, housing cabinets with glass doors. A commercial-style duel fuel range creates a focal area, which is enhanced by the handmade tile backsplash. The colors of the kitchen were chosen to match the outdoors, and new red oak replaced black-and-white vinyl squares. A subdued, dark green laminate countertop with a wooden edge replaced the bright red one, imparting a more pleasing complement to the design palette. Once completed, the kitchen became the perfect venue for cooking and entertaining, exactly as the family desired. «

DESIGNER
William Cederberg
Cederberg Kitchens & Additions
630 Weaver Dairy Road, Ste. 106
Chapel Hill, NC 27514
919.967.1171

SPECIAL FEATURES
Iroka wood (oil finish) butcher block island countertop; tile backsplash designed by Richard Hawkins, homeowner

DIMENSIONS
14 x 13

PRODUCTS USED
Cabinetry: UltraCraft Golden Maple
Countertops: J. Thompson Iroka Wood butcher block
Sink(s): Franke double undermount, stainless steel
Faucets: Latoscana Firenze
Dishwasher: Bosch Evolution, stainless steel
Oven/cooktop: DCS gas range
Hood: KitchenAid Architect Series, undercabinet, stainless steel
Lighting: Seagull
Refrigerator: KitchenAid, stainless steel

MEMBER OF
SEN DESIGN GROUP

PHOTOGRAPHER: SETH TICE-LEWIS

Cozy and Bright

THIS FAMILY OF FOUR IN DUNWOODY, GEORGIA, wanted to enlarge their existing kitchen and to do so called upon Bette Raburn and the design team of The Interior Motive to create a space of their dreams. After the living room, dining room and kitchen were gutted to make one open floor plan, the next challenge was converting the small rooms into one large space that radiated a cozy atmosphere. The team also had the task of vaulting the ceiling and adding transom windows without disturbing the roof lines or exterior aesthetic.

The homeowners requested a contemporary flair for the kitchen, which would be a standout addition to their traditional-style house. So, with that in mind, the design team began drawing up a plan to meet their every desire. The first solution was to raise the vaulted ceiling and add skylights, providing a wash of fresh, natural lighting. Then, to add some contemporary elements, the team incorporated a glass countertop overhang and a glass backsplash, which sparkle in the redesigned space. In the end, the family was provided a space to cook, entertain and study, and they have even hosted several neighborhood parties in their bright, accommodating design. «

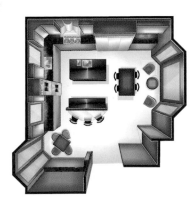

DESIGNER
Bette Raburn ASID
The Interior Motive
6582 Peachtree
Industrial Blvd.
Norcross, GA 30071
770.242.2784

SPECIAL FEATURES
Vaulted ceiling
with skylights; glass
countertop overhang;
glass backsplash

DIMENSIONS
21' x 25'

PRODUCTS USED
Cabinetry: Ultracraft,
Milano Cherry
Flooring: Wood
Countertops: Leopard
wood, island; glass
bartop overhang, island;
granite
Sinks(s): Kohler
Faucets: Hans Grohe
Dishwasher: Fisher &
Paykel
Lighting: Undercabinet;
pendants
Refrigerator: Viking
Oven: KitchenAid
Cooktop: Viking
Warming drawer: Dacor
Ice maker: KitchenAid
Hood: Viking
Wine storage: Sub-Zero

MEMBER OF
SEN DESIGN GROUP

PHOTOGRAPHER: JOEL SILVERMAN

Radical Transformation

THIS HOME, LOCATED IN ALPHARETTA, GEORGIA, is owned by a couple who desired to complete a 12,000-square-foot home tear-down and redo. To make their dreams a reality, the husband and wife duo tasked Bette Raburn ASID of The Interior Motive with the job of redesigning their kitchen. Before beginning the task, Raburn met extensively with the clients to assess their needs and understand their desires.

Both the husband, a commercial builder, and the wife, an artist, desired a large culinary area that would make the best use of space. As parents of two toddlers, they also wanted to create a functional kitchen that would serve their family's needs.

To achieve this, Raburn opened the room and installed two separate islands. The dual islands provide the family with plenty of countertop space. She also lowered the countertop height in an effort to design ergonomically correct proportions for the wife. Bertch custom cabinetry and American walnut flooring add warmth to the room, while the integration of high-end appliances creates the functional kitchen the homeowners desired. «

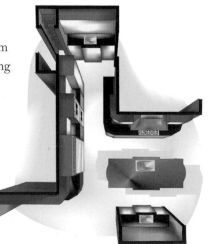

DESIGNER
Bette Raburn ASID
The Interior Motive
6582 Peachtree
Industrial Blvd.
Norcross, GA 30071
404.885.7707

SPECIAL FEATURES
Concrete sink; Kohler
cook sink; wood
countertop; limestone
hood; double islands

DIMENSIONS
29 x 26

PRODUCTS USED
Cabinetry: Bertch
custom
Flooring: American
walnut
Countertops: American
walnut; Caravellas
granite
Sink(s): J. Aaron concrete;
Bella Floret
Pro cook sink: Kohler
Faucet(s): Kohler
Dishwasher: KitchenAid
Cooktop: Wolf
Lighting: Home Waves
Refrigerator: Sub-Zero
Oven: Dacor
Pot filler: Grohe
Coffee maker: Dacor
Past cook sink: Kohler

MEMBER OF
SEN DESIGN GROUP

PHOTOGRAPHER: JOEL SILVERMAN

Sleek and Chic

The duo dwelling in this Atlanta abode includes the wife Carla, an award-winning interior designer with a stellar sense of style. Avid entertainers who also love to cook, Carla and her husband put functionality at the top of their kitchen wish list. They also desired sleek, contemporary quarters to reflect their affinity for modern flair. To realize their dreams, the homeowners tasked Bette Raburn, ASID of The Interior Motive for the job.

Since the kitchen was comprised of two spaces divided by a pair of small walls, the obstacle lay in maintaining functionality within the confines of the dual layout. After gutting the original room, Raburn and her team created two zones to make navigating the space a snap: One includes the food-preparation/cooking area, while the other is home to the refrigerator, sink and built-in Miele coffee system.

Among the room's many special features are the cabinets, which include stainless steel in the main area and oak cabinets with a wenge finish that encase the coffee system and lend a gracious aesthetic to the otherwise modern feel. With its straight lines and minimalistic approach, the sleek space is a sight to behold and provides the homeowners an ideal spot to entertain in style. «

DESIGNER
Bette Raburn ASID
The Interior Motive
6582 Peachtree
Industrial Blvd.
Norcross, GA 30071
404.885.7707

SPECIAL FEATURES
Stainless steel wall cabinets with fluted glass; built-in coffee system

DIMENSIONS
13 x 19

PRODUCTS USED
Cabinetry: Ultracraft
Countertops: Alaskan White granite
Sink(s): Franke
Dishwasher: Fisher & Paykel Dishdrawers
Refrigerator: Sub-Zero
Range: Wolf
Hardware: Richelieu

MEMBER OF
SEN DESIGN GROUP

Modern Hospitality

THE HOMEOWNERS OF THIS Rio Vista Cresskill, New Jersey, dwelling love to entertain. With two children and many family members and friends, they relish the opportunity to host a bevy of guests. Among their favorite places to gather is the family kitchen, so they desired a culinary space that would meet their specifications, while melding with the modern aesthetic of the home.

The residence was a new build, so although the kitchen wasn't antiquated, the couple requested that the layout be rearranged to better suit their needs. Specifically, the existing kitchen was open to the family room, and there wasn't much division between the areas. In an attempt to create two separate rooms that would complement the home's interior and be conducive to entertaining, the homeowners tasked Amir Ilin and his team at Küche+Cucina with the job of redesigning the space.

Ilin and his team began by reworking the floor plan. The revised layout created a sense of connectedness with the family room while maintaining an element of separation. Within the kitchen, the design team constructed a large center island, which features Pedini cabinetry in the Integra line. The additional cabinetry is also Pedini. In an effort to keep the kitchen bright and open, the wall cabinets and the pantry feature glass fronts. Limestone flooring and CaesarStone countertops further emphasize the aesthetic. «

DESIGNER
Amir Ilin
Küche+Cucina
489 Route 17 South
Paramus, NJ 07652
201.261.5221

SPECIAL FEATURES
Large island for meal preparation and seating

DIMENSIONS
29 x 25

PRODUCTS USED
Cabinetry: Pedini, Integra with wenge finish
Flooring: Limestone
Countertops: CaesarStone
Dishwasher: Bosch
Cooktop: Wolf
Refrigerator: Sub-Zero
Oven: Wolf
Sink: Pedini
Faucet: Pedini

MEMBER OF
SEN DESIGN GROUP

Points of View

THIS HOME IN Alamo, California, has an extraordinary view of its vineyard and park-like setting, and, as such, the kitchen needed to provide a full range of functions without blocking any sightlines. The space also needed to be kept open to create a sense of unity between the eating area/conservatory and family room. Marilyn C. Gardunio, CKD, and the design team at J.B. Turner & Sons solved this problem by installing multiple Sub-Zero refrigerator drawers in lieu of a conventional refrigerator, removing much of the upper cabinetry and enlarging the opening between the kitchen and family room. Additionally, the team eliminated a set of windows with a bench seat and replaced them with a sliding French door, which leads to the beautiful outdoor panorama.

Gardunio merged her skills with colorist Leslie Kalish in selecting materials and colors for the project. A softer Provence palette that complements the setting replaced the rustic pine that previously covered the floors, ceilings, and cabinets. In the family room, a slate ledgerock veneer was chosen to replace the heavy river rock fireplace. The floors in this space are now a combination of French limestone and antique wide plank French oak dipped in a gray wash.

Whether they are taking in a beautiful sunset or just watching the grapes ripen on the vines, this family is enjoying the beautiful outdoor scenery that is now a part of their home. «

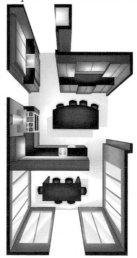

DESIGNER
Marilyn C. Gardunio, CKD
J.B. Turner & Sons
1866 Pleasant Valley Ave.
Oakland, CA 94611
510.658.3441

SPECIAL FEATURES
Roof lantern over the table to create the conservatory ambiance, pantry with wine cellar door featuring aged wood and iron scrolling, three chandeliers

DIMENSIONS
24 x 17

PRODUCTS USED
Cabinetry: Hampshire Cabinetry for perimeter and island, Jay Rambo for bar area
Countertops: Granite, marble, zinc, handcrafted metal
Sink(s): Whitehaus fireclay sink
Faucet: Rohl
Refrigerator: Sub-Zero drawer
Range: LaCornue
Dishwasher: Miele
Liner: Vent-A-Hood
Wine Cooler: Sub-Zero
Lighting: Terzani
Wallcovering: Venetian plaster

MEMBER OF
SEN DESIGN GROUP

PHOTOGRAPHER: STEVEN PAUL WHITSITT

Designer's Challenge

THIS KITCHEN IS in a new home in Statesboro, Georgia, and was a special opportunity for A Contemporary Cupboard, as it not only is located in a model home but is also owned by the home's designer, Lynda Williamson, and her family.

The biggest challenge this kitchen presented was its streamlined nature. Williamson envisioned a large, open area for cooking, accompanied by clean lines and the absence of upper cabinetry. She loves to entertain, and while she was accustomed to a large island, she wanted an even bigger one in her new home! To solve this design challenge, designer Kim Grantham of A Contemporary Cupboard paid particular attention to the organization of the owners' belongings, as each cabinet was carefully placed with a specific function or purpose in mind. A few examples of the new-and-improved storage suite include roll-out shelving, lift-up mixer shelves, a pull-out spice rack, and numerous drawer stacks. To give the cabinetry its refined, clean appearance, Grantham incorporated a slab-style door with inset application into the design.

The butler's pantry design uses a combination of stacked cabinets and abundant shelving to efficiently house all the owners' platters, trays, sets of china, and assorted partyware. Its spacious breakfast/coffee bar provides plenty of storage for morning necessities. Adding a final touch of warmth, the slate floor plays off the blue-gray hues of this magnificent kitchen. «

DESIGNER
Kim Grantham
A Contemporary
Cupboard
721 S. Main St., Suite 11
Statesboro, GA 30458
912.681.1181

SPECIAL FEATURES
Large island for maximum storage, built-in niches for appliances

DIMENSIONS
43 x 16

PRODUCTS USED
Cabinetry: Bertch Custom
Flooring: Slate
Countertops: Corian
Sink(s): Blanco
Faucet(s): Kohler
Cooktop: Gaggenau
Oven(s): Gaggenau
Refrigerator: Gagggenau
Microwave: Sharp
Warming Drawer: Gaggenau
Dishwasher: Gaggenau
Icemaker: GE

MEMBER OF
SEN DESIGN GROUP

Grand Openings

SADDLED WITH A 1950s kitchen, this Ventura, California, family was overdue for a remodel. Designer Ronni Fryman of Kitchen Places suggested opening up the space to the dining and living areas to create a more contemporary environment.

The owners fell in love with slab-style cabinetry faced in Zebrano, a laminate that resembles zebrawood, and asked for the veneers to be applied horizontally. While most would shy away from this unconventional and possibly busy aesthetic, it is the addition of other patterns that contributes to the success of this design. Oak panels stained in a dark brown color allow the grain's texture to show through, anchor the cabinet ends, and function as floating shelves with flush lighting. The tile floors have a very subtle color variation, but more motion is created with various sized tiles and grout lines.

Sparkling accents include stainless steel appliances; aluminum-framed, frosted-glass doors that are illuminated from within; and a glass-tile backsplash that reinforces the horizontal aesthetic. And since both husband and wife occasionally work from home, a second work space was created in the kitchen.

The family's favorite part of the remodeling project is the openness, which allows them to celebrate backyard barbecues, dinnertime conversations, televised sports activities, and business tasks—all within the same, compartmentalized space. «

DESIGNER
Ronni Fryman
Kitchen Places
4125 Market St., #1
Ventura, CA 93003
805.658.0440

SPECIAL FEATURES
Glass-tile backsplash, custom-width cabinets that provide equally sized doors

DIMENSIONS
9 x 19

PRODUCTS USED
Cabinetry: Amero Cabinet Collection by Pacific Crest Industries
Flooring: Casa Dolce Casa porcelain tile
Countertops: CaesarStone in Lagos Blue
Sink(s): Kohler
Faucets: Kohler
Dishwasher: KitchenAid
Range: KitchenAid
Refrigerator: KitchenAid
Wallcovering: MDC Wallcoverings, Tech-Wall, Maharam fabrics
Warming Drawer: KitchenAid
Microwave: KitchenAid
Wine Cooler: GE Monogram
Backsplash: Casa Dolce Casa glass mosaic tile
Cabinet Hardware: Richelieu wood, Top Knobs stainless steel
Refrigerator Pulls: Top Knobs
Barstools and Furniture: Neuvié
Interior Design: Monica Gear

MEMBER OF

SEN DESIGN GROUP

PHOTOGRAPHER: ©SCHAFPHOTO

Penthouse View

HISTORICAL ELEMENTS AND modern amenities combine in this luxurious renovated penthouse. The galley kitchen, designed by Anita Kealey of The Design Studio, Inc., was made for multiple people to work without interrupting each other's work flow.

The kitchen is just as sensible as it is beautiful. The Dacor six-burner gas cooktop, the electric double convection oven and the warming drawer maximize efficiency. Twenty-four-inch tiles line the floor, and the tin ceiling mimics that original to the building. The backsplash above the CaesarStone counters is enhanced with warm-toned horizontal deco tiles.

The commercial-style deep stainless steel sink is complemented by an industrial spray faucet. The bar sink is partnered with a trough sink that doubles as an ice bucket for entertaining. These details are a timeless marriage of historic form and modern function. The breakfast booth is reproduced to follow the art form of the classic Barcelona chairs in the den. The counter bar front is covered with black leather-stitched squares that follow a consistent theme. The quarter-sawn oak cabinetry is repeated in the Italian steam-bent hydraulic bar stools. The look of warm woods, reeded glass and stainless steel is timeless. «

DESIGNER
Anita Kealey
The Design Studio Inc.
123 S. Main Ave., Ste. 200
Sioux Falls, SD 57104
605.336.6061

SPECIAL FEATURES
10' high ceilings accommodate double height cabinet uppers; ceiling in bar and breakfast booth opens to 18' high, showcasing the massive arched windows.

DIMENSIONS
36' x 9'

PRODUCTS
Cabinetry: StarMark Cabinetry, quarter-sawn red oak, chestnut finish
Refrigerator: Dacor
Double oven: Dacor
Hood: Vent-A-Hood
Warming drawer: Dacor
Microwave: Dacor
Dishwasher: Bosch
Sink(s): Blanco; Kohler
Faucet: Blanco
Hardware: Top Knobs
Countertops: Caesar Stone
Flooring: Tile, Tau
Lighting: Oggetti Luce
Banquet: The Design Studio
Seating: Biebe
Beverage cooler: Dacor
Ceiling: M-Boss
Backsplash: Tile, Tau

Fit for a Chef

THIS REMODELED KITCHEN in Douglaston Manor, New York, not only needed a face lift, but was also in dire need of a design to suit the professional cook. Jeff Boico of Kitchen and Bath Center was ready to implement a design good enough for a master chef.

The sink was placed in the center island to allow the cook to spread out in preparation for the many meals and holidays that had her frequently entertaining guests. The refrigerator and oven with the microwave situated above it are conveniently placed on the back wall, opposite the island, so that this cook could be in her own domain without anyone getting underfoot.

The range was placed adjacent to the sink in the island, so that when necessary, there could be two people preparing and cooking in the kitchen. To give this space a sense of uniqueness in its professional-inspired air, hand-carvings are displayed at the ends of the island, an eye-catching window treatment and onlay play up the design, and a custom hand-carved hood looks very distinguished in the completed design. In the end, the cook had a place to entertain guests while preparing a five-star culinary delight. «

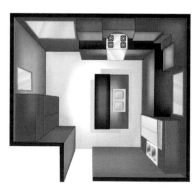

DESIGNER
Jeff Boico CKD
Classic Kitchen and Bath Center
1062 Northern Blvd.
Roslyn, NY 11576
516.621.5500

SPECIAL FEATURES
Multi-level island with hand-carving supports; glass mural tile backsplash; hand-carved hood over range

DIMENSIONS
16 x 18

PRODUCTS USED
Cabinetry: Neff
Flooring: Wood
Countertops: Silestone
Sink(s): Franke
Faucet: Franke
Dishwasher: Miele
Range: Wolf
Refrigerator: Sub-Zero
Wallcovering, ceiling covering: Custom painted by Erik Fennge
Oven: Wolf
Microwave: Wolf

MEMBER OF
SEN DESIGN GROUP

PHOTOGRAPHER: STEVE GERACI

Minimalist Maven

THE DESIGN SKILLS of Classic Kitchen and Bath Center's Jeff Boico highlight this lovely New York kitchen. To achieve a loft-like, open ambiance, Boico removed the wall between the kitchen and dining room. This configuration allows the space to flow as a single working unit. Featuring a new furniture piece with raised glass supported by steel beams, the enhanced area now defines the kitchen's elegant view from the dining area. Coordinating, base cabinetry is also raised with steel legs that impart a contemporary, minimalist furniture-like appearance.

The furniture elements of the space attract the eye, but the functionality draws in the convenience factor. An increased ceiling height of a soaring 14 feet enhances the open ambiance, therefore allowing the kitchen to feel more spacious. A modern, horizontal line is repeated at the thick light bridge and countertops. The definition provided by these facets gives the room strong character. Boico's work resulted in a stunning kitchen suited to impress a range of guests, from friends to family to colleagues. «

DESIGNER
Jeff Boico
Classic Kitchen and Bath Center
1062 Northern Blvd.
Roslyn, NY 11968
516.621.7700

SPECIAL FEATURES
Cabinetry built with steel frames, legs; open loft-like feel; horizontal thick light bridge; furniture island with glass raised on steel posts

DIMENSIONS
21 X 20

PRODUCTS USED
Cabinetry: Neff
Flooring: Bamboo
Countertops: Zodiaq
Sinks: Franke
Faucets: Franke
Dishwasher: Miele
Cooktop: Wolf
Lighting: Recessed 4.5-inch incandescent high hats
Refrigerator: Viking
Wallcovering: Paint
Oven: Miele

MEMBER OF
SEN DESIGN GROUP

PHOTOGRAPHER: STEVE GERACI/REFLEX PHOTO

Wine in the Design

In this townhouse, the client needed two sinks: a large prep sink and a main sink. To accommodate his request, Fara Boico of Classic Kitchen and Bath Center placed the prep sink in the island, which created two workstations with plenty of counter space. The client also needed to maximize storage space, so the designers put shallow cabinets on the back of the island. They also designed a custom hutch for both storage and filing.

The client lives in a townhouse and the windows could not be changed, so the cabinets had to be designed in such a way that they wouldn't protrude and block out the sunlight. The client also wanted areas to display her collectibles. For this, the team designed angled shelves—installed from the wall cabinet to window—which serve as a sunny storage spot and also soften the transition to the windows. Other display areas were added, such as a plate rack in the hutch.

Since the clients were wine collectors, they wanted to incorporate authentic wine labels into the design. To that end, Boico hand-painted labels on the limestone tiles that grace the backsplash. Other pieces of the project that made it truly one of a kind were the grape corbels and onlays, which further play up the vino-inspired theme. «

DESIGNER
Fara Boico
Classic Kitchen and Bath Center
1062 Northern Blvd.
Roslyn, NY 11576
516.621.7700

SPECIAL FEATURES
Custom hutch with file cabinet storage; grape corbels and onlays; island with angled fluted panel

DIMENSIONS
24 x 18

PRODUCTS USED
Flooring: Tuscany tumbled porcelain
Countertops: Granite Crema Bordeaux
Sink(s): Franke
Faucets: Delta Brizo
Dishwasher: Miele
Cooktop: Wolf
Lighting: Hera
Refrigerator: Sub Zero
Oven: Thermador

MEMBER OF
SEN DESIGN GROUP

PHOTOGRAPHER: STEVE GERACI

Fabulous Fusion

SITED SQUARELY IN A SPLENDID SOUTHAMPTON, N.Y., development, this home was in need of a kitchen befitting its alluring locale. Desiring a contiguous blend of contemporary design within their traditional-styled dwelling, the homeowners also wanted a space in which they could entertain their many guests. To satisfy their goals, the owners gave the nod to Rob Taber of Classic Kitchens & Baths.

After completely gutting the existing space, Taber ventured to create an ultra-efficient culinary spot perfectly targeted for cooking and entertaining. Because the clients entertain often, they needed a room with an open flow and feel. They gave Taber creative license to design an eye-catching kitchen.

One challenge: to design a workable room in a not-so-workably shaped space. To overcome this, Taber broke up the kitchen into sections, making each area task-specific. Now the owners have plenty of room to whip up meals for guests and have enough space to store their cookware and other items. The cabinetry presented the other challenge, which Taber met by blending full-overlay cabinets with inset cabinets. A desk in one zone allows for quiet calculation. All told, this eclectic kitchen makes cooking and entertaining an event to remember. «

DESIGNER
Rob Taber
Classic Kitchen & Bath Center Ltd.
1062 Northern Blvd.
Roslyn, NY 11576
516.621.7700

60b Jobs Lane
Southhampton, NY 11968
631.204.9500

SPECIAL FEATURES
Custom color match; combination of full overlay and inset cabinets and two manufacturers

DIMENSIONS
16 x 30

PRODUCTS USED
Cabinetry: Neff Classic
Countertops: Granite, stainless steel
Sink(s): Custom stainless steel
Dishwashers: Miele
Cooktop: Wolf
Refrigerator: Sub-Zero
Oven: Wolf

MEMBER OF
SEN DESIGN GROUP

PHOTOGRAPHER: STEVE GERACI

DESIGNER
Amir J. Ilin
Küche+Cucina
489 Route 17 S.
Paramus, NJ 07652
201.261.5221

268 Main St.
Madison, NJ 07940
973.937.6060

SPECIAL FEATURES
Two islands, each with different levels and counter materials; high-gloss lacquer panels covering two walls; glass doors with high-gloss lacquer doors and panels in a matching color; fully integrated flush handles on ebony cabinets

DIMENSIONS
31 x 29

PRODUCTS USED
Cabinetry: Pedini in Outline and Integra
Flooring: Wood
Countertops: Stainless steel, glass, high-gloss lacquered ebony wood
Sink(s): Pedini, stainless steel
Faucets: Pedini, Billy Pro, and Hi Tech
Refrigerators: Sub-Zero, U-Line undercounter
Cooktop: Scholtes for Pedini
Ovens: Gaggenau
Steamer: Gaggenau
Dishwasher: Gaggenau, Fisher & Paykel
Griddle: Miele
Coffee Maker: Miele
Wallcovering: High-gloss lacquer

MEMBER OF
SEN DESIGN GROUP

Perfectly Positioned

THESE CLIENTS PURCHASED a beautiful horse farm in Tewksbury, New Jersey, and hired architects Tony Kowidge and Joel Ives from IS&L to handle the whole-house redo. For the complete kitchen redesign, the architects knew where to go: Amir Ilin from Küche+Cucina.

The kitchen had a dividing wall between the main kitchen area, so Ilin started the transformation by taking down the wall and opening the kitchen work area. The new scheme allows for a much better flow and creates a bigger cooking space, which now houses the appliances and a prep island. Ilin compensated for the lack of wall space by adding a pair of storage pantries and a custom six-door storage cabinet, using the same finishes as the kitchen. He then positioned them between the kitchen and the living area.

Ilin designed two very unique islands. One is for cooking, with a large, raised, industrial-like stainless steel surface for food preparation. Its lower section boasts a high-gloss lacquer over ebony wood—a warm counterpoint to the stainless steel. The second island is for entertaining, outfitted with five bar stools and a glass counter area. Lastly, Ilin inserted three ovens and a coffee maker in the outside wall of the walk-in pantry. The new kitchen was now ready for a cup of espresso or an Italian feast. «

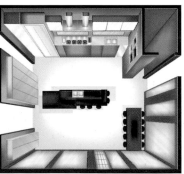

If you like **Best of Signature Kitchens,** look for these
and other fine **Creative Homeowner books** wherever books are sold.

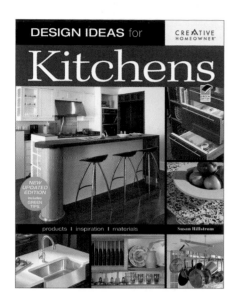

Design Ideas for Kitchens
Design inspiration for creating a new and
improved kitchen. Over 500 photos.
224 pp.; 8½" x 10⅞"
BOOK #279412

REVISED AND EXPANDED

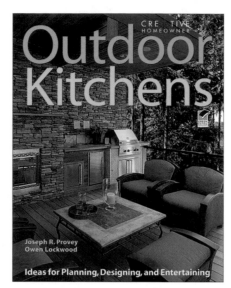

Outdoor Kitchens
Planning and design advice from top
professionals. Over 335 photos.
224 pp.; 8½" x 10⅞"
BOOK #277571

Natural Style
Interior design with eco-friendly materials.
Over 200 photos.
208 pp.; 8½" x 10⅞"
BOOK #279062

Dream Log Homes and Plans
Great ideas for designing, buying, building,
and furnishing an ideal log home.
240 pp.; 9¼" x 10⅞"
BOOK #276158

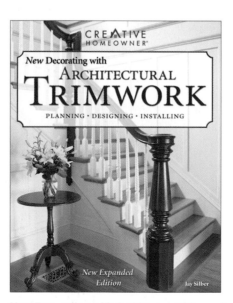

New Decorating with Architectural Trimwork
Transform a room with trimwork. Over 550
color photos and illustrations.
240 pp.; 8½" x 10⅞"
BOOK #277500

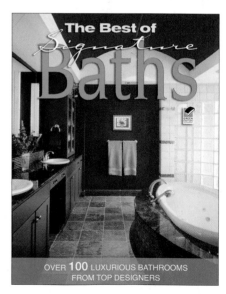

The Best of Signature Baths
Inspiring bathrooms from top designers.
Over 250 photos.
240 pp; 8¼" x 10⅞"
BOOK #279522

For more information and to order direct, go to **www.creativehomeowner.com.**